BRAZIL
Under Cardoso

A Publication of the Americas ✖ Society

BRAZIL

UNDER CARDOSO

EDITED BY
SUSAN KAUFMAN PURCELL
& RIORDAN ROETT

LYNNE
RIENNER
PUBLISHERS

BOULDER
LONDON

Published in the United States of America in 1997 by
Lynne Rienner Publishers, Inc.
1800 30th Street, Boulder, Colorado 80301

and in the United Kingdom by
Lynne Rienner Publishers, Inc.
3 Henrietta Street, Covent Garden, London WC2E 8LU

Library of Congress Cataloging-in-Publication Data
Brazil under Cardoso / edited by Susan Kaufman Purcell and Riordan
  Roett.
      p.   cm.
    Includes bibliographical references (p.) and index.
    ISBN 1-55587-452-5 (pbk. : alk.paper)
    1. Brazil—Politics and government—1985– 2. Brazil—Economic
policy. 3. Brazil—Social policy. 4. Brazil—Foreign relations—
United States. 5. United States—Foreign relations—Brazil.
6. Brazil—Foreign relations—1985– 7. United States—Foreign
relations—1993– I. Purcell, Susan Kaufman. II. Roett, Riordan,
1938–
JL2431.B73   1997
320.981'09'049—dc21   97-13956
                                                                  CIP

British Cataloguing in Publication Data
A Cataloguing in Publication record for this book
is available from the British Library.

Printed and bound in the United States of America

5 4 3 2 1

Contents

Illustrations

Foreword

Brazil today plays an increasingly important role in Latin America. It is the dynamic leader of MERCOSUR, the South American Common Market. It is a primary target for U.S., European, and Asian investment. Its stock market remains highly attractive to emerging-market investors. And its capacity to maintain a relatively open and democratic society, with many social and economic policy questions yet to be resolved, is admirable. The farsighted efforts of President Fernando Henrique Cardoso and his administration to introduce fundamental reforms have great significance both for Brazil and for the hemisphere. All of us wish the Brazilians well in this challenging task.

This book examines both Brazil's achievements since the inauguration of Cardoso as president in early 1995 and the policy issues that must still be resolved. The fact that Brazil's reform efforts are being implemented within a democratic political system means that it has often been difficult to achieve a critical mass in favor of particular policies. At the same time, those reforms that have been secured may prove longer lasting than ones passed in countries where a public consensus was lacking. The success of the *Real* Plan in reducing inflation to a historic low is impressive. The Cardoso administration must now persuade the Brazilian Congress to make some difficult—and unpopular—decisions: to generate further revenues to balance the budget and to move more quickly to privatize top-heavy state corporations. Much also remains to be done to alleviate poverty and improve performance in the areas of health, education, and housing.

Many of the economic reforms being implemented will enable Brazil to take advantage of the new opportunities generated by an increasingly global economy. Changes in Brazil's foreign policy, particularly in its relationship with the United States, are working in the same direction. They parallel a reawakening in Washington to the importance of Brazil as the eighth-largest world economy, whose consolidation of democracy and establishment of a market economy will reverberate throughout the hemisphere. This will

9

help ensure the successful creation of a Free Trade Agreement of the Americas by the year 2005. It is a worthy goal that Brazil, the United States, and their neighbors in the hemisphere will be working hard to achieve in the coming years.

Everett Ellis Briggs,
President, Americas Society

Acknowledgments

This book is the result of the combined efforts of a number of individuals and organizations. We especially would like to thank the members of the study group "Brazil Under Cardoso," who contributed useful information and ideas regarding Brazil's economic reform efforts and the ways in which they are affecting, and are affected by, the political system, the social situation, and the foreign policy making process. We owe special thanks to Albert Fishlow, a discussant at the study group, who graciously agreed to write the chapter on the *Real* Plan after Carlos Langoni had to withdraw as a contributor to the book.

We are particularly grateful to the Brazilian Permanent Mission to the United Nations and to Ambassador Celso Amorim, a former foreign minister of Brazil, for his cooperation and extremely helpful comments on earlier versions of the papers included in the book. Paulo Henrique Amorim also provided excellent suggestions and critiques. We would like to thank Stephanie Crane and Kathlyn Snyder, former assistants to the vice president of the Americas Society, for serving as rapporteurs for the study group and for organizing the study group and preparing the resulting manuscript for publication. Alexander Gross, secretary to the vice president of the Americas Society, and Gladys McCormick, assistant to the vice president of the Americas Society, were very helpful as well in the final stages of the publication process. We also wish to thank Linda Wrigley for editing a portion of the manuscript. Finally, we would like to acknowledge the staff at Lynne Rienner Publishers for their valuable contributions to the editorial and publication process.

This book, and the study group from which it developed, were made possible by a generous grant to the Department of Latin American Affairs of the Americas Society by the Andrew W. Mellon Foundation.

—*Susan Kaufman Purcell*
—*Riordan Roett*

Acronyms and Abbreviations

ARENA	National Renovating Alliance
CIEP-CIAC	Popular Education Integrated Center and Child Assistance Integrated Center
CLT	Consolidation of Labor Laws
EU	European Union
FDI	Foreign Direct Investment
FGTS	Fund for the Guarantee of Workers Security
FTAA	Free Trade Area of the Americas
GDP	Gross Domestic Product
IDESP	Institute of Economic, Social, and Political Studies of São Paulo
INPS	National Social Security Institute
MDB	Brazilian Democratic Movement
MERCOSUR	South American Common Market
MOBRAL	Brazilian Literacy Movement
MST	Landless Rural Workers Movement
NAFTA	North American Free Trade Agreement
PDC	Christian Democratic Party
PDS	Social Democratic Party
PDT	Democratic Workers Party
PFL	Liberal Front Party
PIS/PASEP	Social Integration Programs
PL	Liberal Party
PMDB	Brazilian Democratic Movement Party
PP	Popular Party
PPB	Brazilian Progressive Party
PPR	Progressive Reform Party
PRN	Party of National Reconstruction
PSDB	Brazilian Social Democracy Party
PT	Workers Party
PTB	Brazilian Workers Party
TSE	Superior Electoral Tribunal
URV	Real Unit of Value

BRAZIL

Introduction

Susan Kaufman Purcell & Riordan Roett

With the inauguration of Fernando Henrique Cardoso as Brazil's president on January 1, 1995, renewed attention has been given to the largest country in Latin America. When democracy was restored in 1985, following twenty-one years of military government, it was expected that Brazil would begin to modernize its economy and address many of the outstanding social issues that had been neglected for some time. Three governments from 1985 to 1995—those of José Sarney, Fernando Collor de Mello, and Itamar Franco—attempted some change but often with limited success. Cardoso's government, elected with a large popular mandate, has begun the process of revising the statist 1988 constitution and has given priority to fighting inflation (with the *Real* Plan), downsizing the public sector, and attracting direct foreign investment.

Because the reforms are being implemented under democratic rule, they have required substantial negotiation and compromise between the government and the political and economic elite. The reform process has also focused attention on the need for social changes in order to give the majority of Brazilians a stake in the changing economy. Finally, and to improve the chances that the reforms will endure, the Cardoso administration has sought a more cooperative and mutually beneficial relationship with the United States.

This book offers an assessment of the reform effort in Brazil. It is the result of a study group that met in 1996 under the auspices of the Americas Society. The group comprised individuals from business, journalism, academia, and government. Participants included Brazilians and North Americans. Four essays were written for the group. Although the draft documents were discussed in the meetings of the study group, the final versions of the essays reflect the personal views of the individual authors and not those of the study group itself.

The first chapter addresses the current state of Brazilian politics. Riordan Roett argues that the economic reform process is influenced by the realities of the political environment, which remains locally and regionally oriented. The government needs to bargain with the Congress to achieve its goals, and the fiscal impact of securing support is high. While there is growing public support for introducing market reforms, the political elites do not yet see fit to support fully the goals of the Cardoso administration. Winning a constitutional amendment to allow Cardoso to seek a second term of office should provide an important impetus to accelerating the reform process and allowing Brazil to begin to address longer-term social development questions.

Albert Fishlow examines the *Real* Plan in Chapter 2. Introduced in mid-1994 by Fernando Henrique Cardoso when he served as finance minister in the government of Itamar Franco, the plan achieved spectacular short-term results with a dramatic fall in the rates of inflation. The *Real* Plan is widely recognized, Fishlow comments, as Brazil's most successful effort at stabilization. Now the critical issue is its durability, which will depend fundamentally on the credibility of the administration's fiscal policy and its capacity to address the deficit. While progress is slow, the author believes that the *Real* Plan is likely to succeed.

Chapter 3, by Amaury de Souza, deals with Brazil's social agenda at the end of the century. The author addresses important policy questions, such as income distribution, changing patterns of poverty and inequality, and the critical importance of education. The Cardoso government has committed itself to addressing what the president has termed an "unjust country." To do so will require attention to job creation and employment flexibility, land reform, income redistribution, and compensatory programs for the poorest of the poor. An important element in the administration's program is a total reorganization of the social security system, which is close to bankruptcy. To accomplish the social goals of the government will require political will and a successful implementation of the current economic reform agenda.

Susan Kaufman Purcell considers U.S.-Brazilian relations in Chapter 4. With the end of the Cold War, historical irritants in the bilateral relationship have abated, and the two countries have found a number of issues on which to agree. But the growing convergence of interests between Washington and Brasília does not mean that there are not policy differences. The area of free trade is one in which the Brazilian preference for using Mercosul (the South American Common Market) as a building block for hemisphere-wide integration clashes with the U.S. desire to expand the North American Free Trade Agreement (NAFTA) in order to achieve a Free Trade Area of the Americas (FTAA), as agreed to in Miami in December 1994. Other differences are amenable to negotiation, and there is ample room for collaboration in critical areas such as the environment, drugs, refugee problems, and border disputes.

1

Brazilian Politics at Century's End

Riordan Roett

With the election of Fernando Henrique Cardoso as the first modern chief executive of Brazil in late 1994, there was widespread expectation that his presidency would herald a significant turning point in the modernization of the Brazilian economy.[1] Compared to its neighbors in the hemisphere—Argentina, Chile, and Peru—Brazil was perceived to be lagging in its efforts to introduce a market economy, undertake the privatization of state-owned assets, address fiscal imbalances, and provide the incentives needed for a competitive economy in the twenty-first century.

Following the inauguration on January 1, 1995, the new government appeared to hesitate but finally sent a series of constitutional amendments to the Congress for action. To the surprise of most observers, the government's program moved quickly through the legislature. It was then assumed that 1996 would see a repeat of the successes of the previous year as the Congress turned to the details of actually interpreting and implementing the broad-brush amendments in the economic area and then move on to a second set of priorities. But that expectation has not been realized, and Brazilian politics midway through Cardoso's four-year term of office remains unpredictable and highly contentious—which is why the heralded progress in addressing significant economic policy issues has not occurred.

In large part, the belief that Cardoso would be able to overcome the personalism and populism that have characterized Brazilian politics for decades was based on the stunning success of his *Real* Plan. Announced in March 1994, the plan has actually succeeded in driving levels of inflation down to historic levels. The attack on inflation was accompanied by a modicum of policy reforms during the presidential term of Itamar Franco (1992–1995), who, as vice president, had succeeded Fernando Collor de Mello (1990–1992) in December 1992, following the latter's resignation in the face of imminent impeachment. Franco had selected Cardoso, then a federal senator from São Paulo, as foreign minister and then as finance minister. As finance minister, Cardoso assembled a technocratic team that quickly drew up the bold *Real* Plan. As Cardoso emerged as the favorite precandidate for the 1994 presidential elections, thanks to the initial success of the anti-inflation program, reformers read into his growing popularity the possibility of serious institutional realignment. His victory over Luis Inácio "Lula" da Silva in the October 1994 election (Cardoso won with 34.3 million votes, or 54.4 percent of the valid vote) seemed to confirm that Brazil was ready for change. A defeat for the second time of the spokesman for the left, or public sector–oriented interests in Brazil, could only mean that public opinion, influenced by the economic success of the *Real* Plan, was ready for real economic and political change.

While the *Real* Plan has continued to function, its future is unpredictable because of politics as usual in Brazil, particularly in the Congress. Unless the Cardoso administration is able to convince the Congress of the need for significant fiscal reform, the *Real* Plan may face a bleak future. Key elements in a fiscal package would include a restructuring of the social security system, an updating of the tax collection system, and a significant reduction in the size of the public sector. But the probability of significant fiscal changes is limited by the nature of the Brazilian political system.

To show why politics hinders economic progress in Brazil, this essay examines the nature of the political party system, the state and local bases of political power in Brazil, the interests that represent the status quo in Brazil, and the prospects for additional reform in the Cardoso administration. The first three factors provide insight into the highly fluid, nonideological and nonprogrammatic nature of the political process. Moreover, they offer a realistic perspective of how difficult it is—and will be—to move the economic and social agenda forward without political reform.

It is important to point out that words such as *immobilism* and *stalemate* are inappropriate in describing Brazilian politics today. The political process is, as mentioned, highly fluid—new coalitions and alliances are born every day in the Congress. While political commentators may see an immobilized system (by non-Brazilian standards), what functions day to day in Brazil is a system that moves quickly to react to—and to protect—the local and state interests of the incumbent political and economic elites. While it is a dysfunctional system from the perspective of political theory, it is highly functional—and successful—for those interested in maintaining the current balances of power in Brazil. It does not mean that those driving the system are opposed to change; they want change that favors or strengthens their position and their constituencies. From one perspective, this is a rational and functional approach to elections, the process of reform, and the distribution of power. While it precludes major systemic reform, it achieves a precarious consensus among regional elites, who remain the backbone of national politics in Brazil.

THE BRAZILIAN POLITICAL PARTY SYSTEM

Brazilian political parties are best understood as shifting groups of self-interested individuals who find it convenient to come together under a bland banner that usually includes words such as *progressive, social,* or *democratic.* In reality, the form and substance of the particular entity will probably demonstrate little progressiveness in program orientation, a very modest commitment to social reform or change, and manifest impatience with acting democratically.

Brazil did not have a political party system until 1945.[2] The Empire (1822–1889) saw its elites bifurcated into conservative and liberal factions (or parties) that rotated in power and represented postindependence economic and social elite interests. Those interests, given the economic formation of Brazil during the colonial and imperial epochs, were heavily rural and agricultural. Slavery was not abolished until 1888; Brazil's export profile was composed primarily of agricultural crops well into the twentieth century.

With the peaceful overthrow of the Empire in 1889, the Old Republic (1889-1930) witnessed a convergence of local and provincial factional interests. One national conservative party—

the only significant political organization in this period—served as an umbrella organization for elite control. It was driven by the economic interests of the two most powerful states in the federation, São Paulo and Minas Gerais. Decentralization in Brazil was profound: state governors were titled presidents, and the states were able to impose taxes and raise their own armies. Getúlio Vargas's seizure of power in 1930 resulted in a confusing period in which a number of local and state political organizations appeared. A product of the regional political elite in the southern state of Rio Grande do Sul, Vargas had lost the 1930 presidential election, which was marred by widespread fraud. With the support of disaffected military officers, his own state's political leadership, many of the poor northeastern states, and the important state of Minas Gerais (which had been denied the presidential nomination by the São Paulo oligarchy), he launched an offensive against the Old Republic in late 1930. The incumbent president, Washington Luis, resigned, and Vargas arrived in Rio de Janeiro in October to become provisional president. The 1930–1945 period was one of confusion, and a superficial political pluralism ended with the establishment of the protofascist New State in 1937. After Vargas was deposed by the armed forces in 1945, political elites subdivided into pro- and anti-Vargas forces. The principal parties or groups that dominated the 1946 Republic (1946–1964) generally supported a national-populist set of development policies, characterized by import substitution industrialization, the nationalization of the oil industry, and the growth of the urban labor movement. But the system was dominated by the office and the personality of the president. By 1964, the party system of 1946 consisted of thirteen loosely structured organizations, many of which were splinters of three larger political groupings that had been formed in 1945.

By the early 1960s, the Brazilian political system began to polarize. The post-1945 import-substitution-industrialization model had resulted in economic inefficiencies, a lack of competitiveness, and steadily rising inflation. Direct foreign investment was flat. Social tensions, resulting from the rapid urbanization of Brazil after 1945, and increasing pressure from rural groups for land reform created a climate of violence and suspicion. The military, which saw themselves as the guardians of the Brazilian state, were concerned that groups on the left were exploiting the rising tide of frustration and might actually resort to force to accomplish their reform agenda. To preclude such a situation, the military

moved in late March 1964—with the support of the business community, much of the middle class, and the traditional elites—to
close the system.

The military intervention of 1964 resulted in a purge of the
existing political system, with many of the old leaders losing their
political rights for a decade. After a halfhearted effort to work
within the old party framework, the military leadership abolished
the pre-1964 system and created two parties, with ARENA
(National Renovating Alliance) representing pro-regime tenden-
cies and the MDB (Brazilian Democratic Movement) representing
what remained of the left and the antimilitary political actors.
ARENA, with strong support from the military presidents, com-
manded an absolute majority in Congress until 1979. But throughout the military period, ARENA was riven with regional and factional disputes. The MDB, on the other hand, fragmented into a
variety of ideological subgroups defined by their willingness or
not to play by the military-established rules of the game.

By the late 1970s, there was widespread discontent with the
false dichotomy of the two-party system. In 1979, the Congress
approved a government plan to abolish ARENA and the MDB
and to permit renewed party pluralism. The MDB became the
PMDB (Brazilian Democratic Movement Party); ARENA changed
its name to the Social Democratic Party (PDS) but fared badly at
the polls and, in 1993, joined with the small Christian Democratic
Party (PDC) to establish the Progressive Reform Party (PPR). A
Popular Party (PP) was organized for a short period of time by
MDB centrists and ARENA progressives but soon merged with
the PMDB; the Liberal Front Party (PFL), with its electoral base
primarily in the conservative northeast, was formed in 1984. The
PFL joined the PMDB in 1984–1985 to guarantee the indirect election in January 1985 (in an electoral college) of Tancredo Neves;
smaller, more traditional parties also appeared in the mid-1980s.

Perhaps the most significant development after 1979 was the
establishment of the class-based Workers Party (PT), a new mili-
tant organization based originally on the emerging power of the
new unionism that reflected Brazil's impressive industrial growth
after 1964. The new unionism was an effort by a younger generation of industrial workers to gain independence from the traditional control of the Labor Ministry and the complex bureaucracy
of labor courts created in the early 1940s. The rapid expansion of
the Brazilian economy after 1964 created a large, better educated,
and more aggressive working class—concentrated in São Paulo

but with strong support throughout the states of the southeast—that used confrontation with the military regime as one mechanism for achieving their goals.

The new unionists became a critical element in the widespread mobilization of civil society in the early 1980s, which attempted to convince the military regime to hold direct elections for president in 1985. While that undertaking failed to win congressional approval because of pressure from the military regime, the nationwide campaign gave the PT—and Lula—legitimacy, which was used to further the goals of the new unionism in the succeeding decade. While Lula has lost the last two presidential races—to Fernando Collor de Mello and Fernando Henrique Cardoso—the party has continued to expand its electoral base. It performed well in the October 1996 municipal elections and is expected to do so again in the next congressional and gubernatorial elections in 1998.

Legislation in 1985, after the restoration of civilian government, liberalized the requirements for creating new parties. In 1985, there were eleven parties with national registration and representation in Congress, nineteen in 1991, and eighteen in 1995–1996. The most important parties in the Chamber and the Senate continue to be the PMDB, PFL, PSDB, and PPR, all of which represent traditional sources of local and state power in the Brazilian federation. Each of the parties is either headed by or heavily influenced by relatively traditional political leaders. For example, Paulo Maluf, the former mayor of São Paulo, leads the PPR (he is also a former governor and mayor, and former—and possible future—presidential candidate); the PMDB is headed by the former president of the federal Senate, former president José Sarney, who pretends to a second term of office in 1999; and Senator Antônio Carlos Magalhães of Bahia, whose son, Luis Eduardo, served as speaker of the house in the Chamber of Deputies from 1994 to early 1997, is a titan in the PFL.

The first government to follow the twenty-one years of authoritarian rule was dominated by the PMDB, the successor to the principal opposition party during the military period. A lone source of dissent during the military years in national politics, the party carried the banner for a restoration of civilian government when the military regime decided on a policy of gradual opening. That policy decision resulted from a desire to curb the intelligence and security apparatus, which had grown rapidly since 1964. It was driven by an increasingly autonomous labor union movement that demanded a greater share of the pie than had been given to it during the height of the authoritarian government. And civil society—lawyers, professors and students, professional groups, and many in the private sector—lobbied for a termination of military rule and a return to a democratic state. After a period of uncertainty as to whether the armed forces would accept an opposition president in 1985, the PMDB and the PFL put together a ticket for the indirect vote in the electoral college that was acceptable and not seen as a threat by the military. In early 1985, the college met and the candidate of the regime was defeated.

A weak president, José Sarney, succeeded Tancredo Neves after his untimely death in early 1985. A leading figure of the military regime until the very end, when he deserted to join the opposition coalition as its vice-presidential candidate, Sarney reigned as a figurehead chief executive until 1990. The new constitution of 1988, a regressive, populist document, created a time bomb in national politics by transferring a significant share of national income to the states and municipalities, while leaving responsibility for major social programs with the federal government, which now had vastly reduced revenues. The thinking of the populist-dominated Constituent Assembly was that this measure would rebalance power within the federation after two decades of progressive centralization in the hands of the federal government in Brasília. What it actually did was to open the floodgates for local corruption and mismanagement as local and state authorities enjoyed a financial bonanza without any programmatic responsibilities in critical areas of social investment.

The 1988 document confirmed a process that had escalated over the years. Since the mid-1970s, the states and municipalities had increased their share of tax revenues; in 1975, they received 5 percent each of income tax revenues and the tax on manufactured goods. By 1980, these shares had increased to 14 percent and 17 percent, respectively. The new constitution made it a requirement for the federal government to transfer 21.5 percent of the income tax and manufactured goods tax by 1993.

The failure of the *Cruzado* Plan, the Sarney government's 1986 heterodox shock program (which included a general price freeze, a wage freeze, a wage escalation system, and the creation of a new currency), destroyed the credibility of the administration—and by extension that of the PMDB-dominated Congress and the PMDB governors who had been elected at the end of 1986, running on the earlier, euphoric popularity of the *Cruzado*

Plan. The remainder of Sarney's administration was marked by desperate and unsuccessful efforts to control inflation and prices. A relative unknown, Fernando Collor de Mello, the scion of a disreputable state-based oligarchy in the northeastern state of Alagoas, capitalized on national discontent with the traditional parties and organized the Party of National Reconstruction (PRN).

Collor defeated Lula of the Workers Party in the 1989 presidential election, but his party fared poorly. Even after the congressional elections of October 1990, following Collor's inauguration earlier in the year, the party held only twenty seats in the Chamber of Deputies and two Senate seats. In spite of uncertain political support, Collor proceeded with a set of audacious and controversial economic and financial reforms. Among the most successful were the liberalization of trade and the beginnings of the privatization of state assets. As the government appeared to be regrouping in mid-1992, a major crisis erupted, with the president and his chief fund-raiser accused of massive fraud and extortion. Reform efforts ended as the embattled president attempted to avoid impeachment proceedings in the Congress. Public opinion, aroused by the corruption charges and the president's seeming indifference, took to the streets in a wave of peaceful demonstrations calling for him to step down. After a long congressional investigation, impeachment proceedings were initiated, and Collor resigned in December 1992 just before the final vote, which carried by a wide margin.

As part of the constant reshuffling of party allegiances, the PMDB split in 1988 and a center-left splinter group organized the Brazilian Social Democracy Party (PSDB). Among its prominent founders were two São Paulo federal senators, Fernando Henrique Cardoso and Mario Covas (now the PSDB governor of the state). With the resignation of Collor de Mello, the new president, Itamar Franco, restructured the governing coalition and offered three ministries to the PSDB, including the post of foreign relations head to Senator Cardoso. In May 1993, Cardoso moved to the Finance Ministry from which he launched the *Real* Plan in March 1994. With the plan's success—its principal achievement was the dramatic drop in inflation rates—Cardoso was nominated for president; he chose as his vice president Senator Marco Maciel of the PFL. The Cardoso-Maciel ticket easily defeated the PT ticket in late 1994, with Lula again the party's nominee. Cardoso's margin of victory was sufficiently large

(54.4 percent of the valid vote) to avoid a second round of voting in November.

Fernando Henrique Cardoso had a well-established reputation as both an intellectual and a politician when he won the presidency. He had been a professor at the University of São Paulo, and after the military coup of 1964, he left Brazil for Chile, where he coauthored the once influential theory of dependency—the underdeveloped countries are manipulated by the wealthier industrial states—before moving to Paris, where he taught at the University of Paris. Returning to São Paulo in 1968, he conducted research and wrote extensively on development issues. Cardoso ran for the Senate in 1978 on the MDB ticket and served as the alternate to Franco Montoro. When the latter was elected São Paulo state governor in 1982, Cardoso took his place in the federal Senate. He was reelected in 1986 (after a narrow defeat in a race for mayor of São Paulo) and served as government leader in Congress during the Sarney administration. He quickly assumed the role of a superminister in the government of Itamar Franco in 1992–1993, from which he launched his successful drive for the presidency.

The Cardoso government took office in January 1995 and quickly won the support of a number of other political parties as the new regime began its effort to amend the 1988 constitution and to further liberalize the national economy by opening areas such as petroleum, mining, and telecommunications to private investment. The principal goal was to reduce the role of the state in the economy and increase the competitiveness and efficiency of domestic industry. The government succeeded in winning relatively rapid approval of constitutional amendments in key areas of the economy in 1995, but since then, progress has been disappointing in achieving either further constitutional reform or the ordinary legislation required to implement and activate the constitutional changes of 1995. It is one of the ironies of the Cardoso government that the PSDB, the president's party, has been reluctant to support many of his initiatives because they will impact negatively on the natural constituencies of the party. Another irony is the strong support given to the Cardoso program by the PFL, a northeast-based party of regional notables, which supports economic liberalization and market reforms while remaining highly skeptical of political institutional changes. The economic philosophy of the party favors the modernization of the national economy, competitiveness, and increased foreign investment; but the leadership does not appear to see any linkage between a more efficient and productive economy and the probable need for more democratic and representative institutions in Brazil. In many countries experiencing rapid economic change, there is a concomitant desire for greater political participation as individual citizens' stake in the economy—and society—expands.

In the current Brazilian political system, it does not seem incongruous for President Cardoso to be supported by a heterogeneous coalition that is programmatically dominated by the PFL. The Cardoso program offers the PFL what it wants and what works for it and its constituents. The party that purports to be progressive, Cardoso's own PSDB, is equivocal about its enthusiasm for market reforms and remains vaguely wedded to a social democratic concept of a mixed economy in which the government continues to play a strategic role. It is also true that key PSDB legislators are beholden to the rust belt industries of São Paulo state, which fear economic liberalization and the competition that will inevitably impact on their capacity to perform. The other parties in the current governing coalition, the PMDB, Brazilian Progressive Party (PPB), PTB, and PL, represent a broad spectrum of personal and party positions that are determined by state and local interests. These are best understood in terms of the rewards or perks they can extract from the federal government in exchange for their votes in Congress issue by issue.

Thus, a reform-minded president—Cardoso—is only intermittently supported by his own party, which advertises itself as a social democratic alternative for Brazil but lacks the conscience to vote for far-reaching reforms to modernize Brazilian society; the most powerful conservative group, the PFL, representing the most traditional social interests in the country, is the principal advocate of market-oriented reforms. And the remaining members of the more-or-less majority coalition calculate their support for reform in terms of the patronage forthcoming from the embattled central government. This state of affairs stems in large part from the nature of the electoral system and the local and state emphases in Brazilian politics that have dominated since independence in 1822.

BRAZIL'S ELECTORAL SYSTEM AND LOCAL POWER

The political party system since 1985 has been plagued with frequent changes of party affiliation, overtly opportunistic and often short-term party alliances, and a lack of credible national leadership. In addition to the problems created by state and local loyalties, there are certain characteristics of the electoral system in Brazil that help determine the nature of today's party dynamics. Brazil's federal deputies (and municipal council members) are elected by a system of open-list proportional representation.[3] Each state in the federation serves as a single, at-large, multimember voting district. The number of seats per state ranges from eight to seventy, with small states deliberately overrepresented and the large states, such as São Paulo and Minas Gerais, deliberately underrepresented. Successive governments have opted to favor overrepresentation for the smaller, more marginal states as a way of compensating for the economic power and influence of the larger members of the federation. On election day, the voters cast their single ballots either for the party label—in which case their vote merely is added to the party's total vote at the end of the day—or for individual candidates. But the names of party candidates are not listed on the ballots; instead, the voter must write in the candidate's name or registration number. After the balloting has ended, officials determine how many votes each party has received and then determine which party members, based on their total vote, will receive one of the proportionally distributed seats in the legislature.

Increasingly, party coalitions have become critical components in the electoral process.[4] In the 1994 elections, close to half of federal deputies were elected by coalitions. In Brazil, coalition partners lose their party identity and compete in a single basket of votes, which further weakens the political party system. Thus voters have little idea of, or interest in, the party affiliation of candidates. And since campaigns are so individualized (many candidates never mention their party label in their propaganda), the party vote is very small—with the exception of the PT.

A good example in the 1996 municipal election was that of Recife, the capital city of Pernambuco in the Brazilian northeast. A Popular Front alliance composed of seven parties supported the candidacy of federal deputy Humberto Costa. The ideological spectrum of the alliance ran from the two communist parties of Brazil to the region's most conservative, but ideology was not the issue. Costa's voter appeal and the rewards for the parties from his election were sufficient to bring the parties, momentarily, together. Voters vote for the alliance, not the parties. And the leaders of the parties will be available in three years to reconnoiter and position themselves for the next round of congressional, gubernatorial, and presidential voting with little regard to the position they took in 1996—nor would anyone in Brazilian politics expect them to act differently.

Because everyone is elected at large—Brazil does not have local constituencies—a candidate needs to campaign across his state. This system means that candidates aligned with a particular party are running against each other in the lead-up to the election to be sure that they receive a sufficiently large number of votes to qualify for a seat when the positions are proportionally distributed. This defeats any effort at party coherence or program stability. Candidates prefer weak parties that will give them leeway in establishing bases of political support in the state or city. And while some candidates may have special electoral areas in which they seek most of their votes, many others seek votes across the state. This limits, or eliminates, constituent accountability after the elections. In the absence of districts, it is impossible for a citizen to claim one deputy or council member as his or her representative. In turn, the system liberates the newly elected representative from having to maintain the fiction of representation. He or she represents not the voters but the groups and party structures that turned out the vote to guarantee his or her seat at the end of the day.

The situation is aggravated by the ease with which a group can legally organize a party. After 1985, provisional organization of new entities required only that 101 prospective members sign a petition with bylaws, statutes, and program, which are then registered with the Superior Electoral Tribunal (TSE). Permanent registration is somewhat more complicated. Within a twelve-month period, the new party must organize state directorates in nine states and in one-third of the municipalities in each of these states. In 1989, twenty-two parties were able to register candidates for the presidential voting, but in 1994 only nine were registered.

Efforts to revise the 1988 constitution in 1993–1994 contained important proposals to establish a rigid German-style threshold of 3–5 percent of the national vote in order to elect representatives to Congress. These proposals, and many others, were either rejected or tabled by the Congress, whose members had little interest in restricting the expansion of parties in the political process. Other pending changes to the party system languish in the Congress, and the expectation that they will move to the floor is very limited.

Thus, parties begin at the base as weak organizations, vehicles for intermittent electoral purposes. There is little thought to continuity in either program or leadership. Local and state rivalries will drive prominent personalities from one party to another. Peculiar alliances will emerge that represent personalist and local interests. For example, in the October 1996 municipal elections, the PSDB and the PFL (national coalition partners) ran separate mayoral candidates in twenty-one of the twenty-six state capitals and opposed each other in about 90 percent of all municipal posts to be elected in the key states of the south. The PMDB, a nominal member of the Cardoso coalition, ran its own mayoral candidates in twenty state capitals. And the PPB opposed the PSDB in twenty-one cities and the PFL in eighteen. But in the city of São Paulo, a critical arena for the government, the PSDB had its own candidate, and its partner, the PFL, endorsed the PPB candidate.

The localism of politics is further illustrated by the proliferation of mayoralities—there were 4,300 in 1988, 4,974 in 1992, and 5,100 in 1996. New municipal districts are established by the Congress in Brasília. Since many members of Congress consider local office to be far more important than national office, the tendency to support an expansion of the number of municipal positions available every four years is overwhelming (correspondingly, the number of town council positions has increased from 65,000 in 1992 to 70,000 in 1996).

Service in the national Congress is not viewed by most politicians as a permanent career. It is a place in which you spend a four-year term of office to facilitate the transfer of resources back to the state or municipal power structure that sent you to Brasília. To illustrate the point, approximately 116 federal deputies, nearly one-fourth of the Chamber, ran for local office in October 1996. And because individual deputies view national office as transitory, national parties have little meaning. This discourages any sort of party coherence in Brasília. And, in fact, Brazil's political parties tend to be regionally concentrated. The PSDB is highly concentrated in São Paulo and Ceará states; the PT and PPR in São Paulo; the PFL in the northeast; and the Democratic Workers Party (PDT) in Rio de Janeiro and Rio Grande do Sul. These concentrations reflect personalities, local political culture, and historical alliances among local elites.

The long historical development of the party process in Brazil leads to one conclusion: the base of power in Brazil is local. Since local leaders exercise tremendous influence over voter preferences, particularly in the rural areas where illiteracy remains high, a local base of support yields a high degree of influence over those who are elected to the Chamber every four years. The system produces negative effects for the legislative process in Brasília. High turnover rates, especially in the south and southeast, produce deputies with little experience and less interest in getting to know the game. They have private sector or professional options and are often frustrated by a process in Brasília that is usually dominated by the conservative northern and northeastern elites (note, again, that the two leaders of the houses of Congress in 1995–1996 were from the north [Sarney] and the northeast [Magalhães]). It also reduces the interest of the deputies in investing in legislative expertise or in strengthening the institutional procedures of the Congress. Committees are insignificant; hearings are superficial. Members of Congress have one principal job: to funnel as much patronage—or pork—back home as they can in four years in Brasília. This fact of life means that lobbying the executive branch for handouts is more important than legislating, although final congressional approval will be needed for the omnibus bills administered by the federal bureaucracy. A highly prized designation in Brasília is that of minister; federal deputies and senators are allowed to take a leave of absence from the Congress to serve in the executive branch, which facilitates the flow of largesse between Brasília and the states and municipalities. The realities of power in Brasília have been enhanced dramatically since 1988, with the revenue transfers to the states and cities mandated in the constitution.[5]

A 1996 public opinion poll produced by the respected JB-Vox Populi organization confirmed that the National Congress received only a 17 percent approval rating—second lowest of the thirteen institutions rated in the poll. The ratings for the municipal councils in the eight capital cities surveyed were correspondingly low. The three highest institutions in ratings were the national press, the Catholic church, and the armed forces. But this trend is not new. Nor does it appear to have any apparent impact on voter preference at the polls; by a vast majority, traditional political party candidates were voted into, or returned to, office in October. Brazilians apparently believe that they have little control either over the political system as a whole or over individual politicians. It may be that they accept politics as it is or that the constant changes of government have created cynicism about the impact on politics of the individual voter.

POLITICS AND SOCIETY IN CARDOSO'S BRAZIL

The political process does not function in a vacuum in any society. As Brazil enters the twenty-first century, politics needs to be put in the context of Brazilian society and Brazil's social problems. The political class in Brazil represents a highly heterogeneous population of some 170 million people. While the Brazilian economy has changed dramatically in the last twenty-five years, most observers agree that there has been a lag in social development. Twenty percent of Brazilians still live in rural areas, in contrast to 12 percent in Argentina and Chile. Illiteracy stands at 19 percent of the population compared with 13 percent in Colombia and 5 percent in Argentina. Life expectancy at birth is 66.6 years in Brazil; it is 71.9 in Venezuela and 72.3 in Argentina. The infant mortality rate (per 1,000 live births) is high—57.0; it is 36.4 in Colombia and 35.4 in Mexico.

Education, critical to social mobility and professional success, is poor in Brazil, particularly at the primary level where there is a high incidence of repeating class years by those students unable to meet minimum standards. Secondary schools tend to favor pre-university training in a society where the few who attend university are generally from the middle and upper-middle classes. Fernando Henrique Cardoso has stated that he would like to make educational improvement a key goal of his presidency, but he is hampered by budgetary considerations and a backlog of unresolved problems, ranging from inadequate physical infrastructure to poorly paid teachers and high degrees of absenteeism and dropouts by students in the early school years.

Brazil is also very heterogeneous in racial composition. Some 69.6 million people were classified as being of African background in the 1991 national census. That people of color tend to be poorer and less educated in Brazil is a social issue that has long been ignored by the educated population. The country's indigenous population probably stands at about a quarter million and has become the source of international concern as development patterns have impinged on their lands in the northern and northwestern states. Immigrants have always been welcome in Brazil, and there are large communities of descendants of Japanese, Lebanese, Italian, German, and Polish settlers. While the Roman Catholic Church is accepted as the church of preference of the vast majority of Brazilians, Afro-Brazilian religions, popular

Catholicism, Protestantism, and evangelical groups have made a strong impact across the country.

The World Bank and other institutions monitoring economic growth patterns have stated that Brazil's income distribution is highly uneven and ranks among the worst in the world. A small percentage of the population takes home a large share of national income, and the majority receives a very small percentage. This is aggravated by many years of inflation, which impacts most harshly on the poor. Poor economic performance in Brazil for a number of years has punished the working class; the economy in some years produced few new jobs. And the restructuring of Brazilian industry in recent years has led to a reduction in jobs and wage levels in many businesses. Successive governments have failed to find adequate policies to bring about a more equitable distribution of income. This is linked to the widespread poverty in the large cities and the countryside, to the misapplication of public resources for needed social services, and to the attitude among many in the political class that social marginalization and poverty are inevitable in developing countries like Brazil and that there is little government or public policy can do to alleviate the plight of the marginal in society.

These factors need to be considered in analyzing the workings of the Brazilian political system and the need for reform. The agenda of economic reform that has stalled in the Congress should result in an increase in taxes and government revenues from privatization, for example, to generate revenues that would be available for social investment. A reform of the social security system—perhaps along the lines of Chile and Argentina, where the programs have been privatized—would generate internal savings and give individuals a broad stake in the economy. But a political decision will need to be made regarding the distribution of responsibility for social investment in education, health, and housing, given the current distribution of revenues mandated by the 1988 constitution. That is a public policy challenge the Brazilian government hopes to begin to address by the end of the century. The role of politics should be to maximize the individual's freedom to pursue his or her personal and professional interests with the adequate tools to do so. Education, health, and housing are among those tools that are lacking for a large number of Brazilians. The long-range goal of the Cardoso administration is to restructure the economy to make it more efficient and more competitive. That should then provide the means to attack the long-neglected social problems in Brazil. But until the political parties in Congress take that challenge seriously, appropriate responses to societal needs will inevitably be postponed.

THE FUTURE OF THE REFORM
PROCESS IN THE CARDOSO GOVERNMENT

In 1997, at the midpoint of his four-year term of office, President Cardoso finds his government in a position similar to that of all of his democratic predecessors after 1946: how to convince the national Congress of the need to support a reasonable program of reforms? Cardoso's coalition consists of six parties. The conduct of those parties in the Chamber of Deputies is most important in considering the fate of reform proposals. The Senate tends to be more supportive of the administration. The breakdown by seats of the coalition is as follows:

	Chamber (total=531)	Senate (total=81)
PMDB	102	24
PFL	97	22
PSDB	76	14
PPB	88	5
PTB	28	4
PL	9	0

The government coalition holds a slim voting margin in the Chamber. But time and again the president's program has been watered down, overlooked, or defeated. Part of the problem is the cumbersome procedure for reform established in the 1988 constitution. Amendments to the document require two votes by majorities of 60 percent in both houses of Congress. The process originates in the House and continues in the Senate. The final committee recommendation on a constitutional issue needs to be voted by the full membership of each house in two sessions separated by an interval of five sessions.

When Cardoso took office in January 1995, he inherited a lame-duck Congress; the new legislature, elected at the end of 1994, did not take office until February 1995. The government had little hope of passing any new legislation before that date. But even with the swearing-in of the new Congress, in which the government allegedly held a majority, no progress was made. Following the president's successful visit to the United States in April 1995, he returned to Brasília determined to use the traditional tools of his office—appointments and disbursements—to move his agenda. By June, he had cajoled the Congress into passing five important constitutional amendments, which open the state monopolies on petroleum, telecommunications, electricity, and natural gas distribution to foreign investors and grant equal treatment to foreign firms doing business in Brazil. But passing implementing legislation has moved far more slowly through the Congress. While the constitutional amendments authorized a general liberalization of key sectors of the economy, the specifics of how and when to do so require additional action by the Congress. Following the "Big 5" amendments, the government has proposed a series of phase two reforms, which began in early 1996 with a special session of Congress. The principal areas for legislative action were social security, state (administrative) reform, and tax reform. The Congress, unwilling to take unpopular decisions before the municipal elections in October 1996, made little progress in 1996 in supporting the Cardoso administration's reform agenda.

The results of those elections were inconclusive in predicting future political support for the government. To many observers, Brazilian voters appeared to pick candidates who were committed to "good government," and they often elected officials endorsed by outgoing and successful mayors. In São Paulo, the government candidate, Senator José Serra, lost to a little-known member of the administration of Mayor Paulo Maluf. The mayor's party, the PPB, did well nationwide, winning 20 percent of the total vote. After a strong showing in the first round of elections in October, the PT placed poorly in the second round in November but placed second in total votes, with 18 percent of the votes cast. The core government coalition parties, PFL and PSDB, generally held their own in the balloting. The PMDB suffered some unexpected defeats but remains the largest party in the Chamber of Deputies.

In May 1996, the Cardoso government encountered a dramatic example of the inability of the party system to respond to presidential leadership. Deeply concerned about the fiscal imbalance in the national accounts, the administration hoped to move a major reform of social security through Congress by mid-1996. After careful consultation and debate, the government leadership in Congress brought a comprehensive draft bill to the floor only to see it roundly defeated. The press reaction was sharp and negative. The *Jornal do Brasil's* lead editorial the morning after the vote was entitled "Adeus as Ilusões" (farewell to illusions). The editorial stated that the defeat in the Chamber should force the government to reexamine its relationship with the parties that constituted its parliamentary base. The editorial said that the government, referring to the parties in the putative government alliance,

> cannot count on them in the decisive hours. The promise of support extends only to the interest of each deputy. The lack of conviction begins with the relationship to the party: the deputies understand that nothing matters because the parties are nothing more than electoral lists. . . . Members of parliament take care, exclusively, of their reelection, which is their reason to exist. The corporatist blocs now active in the Congress vote only in favor of the corporatist interests that they represent.[6]

The editorial went on to lament the absence of party loyalty and of a more authentic voting system than that of the proportional one now in place, the large number of parties, and the tyranny of the minorities in the Congress that impede legislative progress on major policy initiatives.

And as *Isto É* magazine pointed out, the vote "was an alliance between the corporatist [public sector oriented] left, candidates for mayor [in the October 1996 election] and parliamentarians disposed to force personal favors from the government."[7] And the following week, the *Jornal do Brasil* reported that the administration, prior to the social security vote, had given in to almost all of the major lobbies in granting concessions—and still lost the vote! And, as the journal indicated, the vast majority of these lobbies are actually included within the government's alleged coalition in the Congress.[8] The rural bloc (Ruralista), made up of 179 deputies, belongs to the PFL, PPB, and PTB; grammar school teachers, represented by 200 members of Congress, mostly belong to the PMDB and the PFL; the business community, represented by 250 members of Congress, is primarily drawn from the PSDB.

This illustrates the dilemma of the government. Prior to the October 1996 local elections, there was little legislative time to consider the priority agenda items. Many members had left Brasília to campaign; others would not make tough decisions that would impact negatively on the electoral base of their party or of their colleagues. Without party loyalty, the leadership has little voice in controlling party votes. The difficulty in moving draft legislation through the Congress was illustrated again in late July 1996, when it was reported that discussions between the government and the Congress had broken down over the critical issue of job stability (or permanency) for public employees. Efforts at compromise failed when members of Congress made it clear that they were unwilling to vote against public employee perks in an election year.[9]

The administration in early 1997 again attempted to introduce civil service reform and again met defeat. After passing a civil service reform bill as a whole on April 16, the Chamber of Deputies began to vote on changes to the bill, all of which were aimed at weakening the civil service cutbacks proposed by the Cardoso administration. Defections from the pro-government coalition were part of the problem. But the principal reason for the measure's defeat was the populist appeal of the Workers Party–sponsored provision that called for the maintenance of generous job stability provisions for low-income government workers. Had the measure been defeated, the government would have been in a position to fire non-specialized workers such as elevator operators and messengers. Now these low-income employees have automatic job stability guarantees and can quite literally maintain their jobs and benefits forever, regardless of change in the labor demands of government departments.

On the day the government lost the vote, President Cardoso was on a visit to Canada. Some argued that the president should have remained in Brasília to lobby for his legislation. Others said that the Chamber president, responsible for conducting the vote, failed to realize that many pro-government deputies were absent from the floor. Either or both explanations may be true, but the overwhelming reason for the success of the measure was its wide political appeal and the unwillingness of the legislators to understand the long-term fiscal implications of the measure. It is expected that the government will be able to achieve some modification of the costly job stability guarantees, but it will be later than the government wanted and the fiscal impact will be far slighter than planned.

While attempting to gain approval for its legislative agenda in 1997, the key policy issue to emerge was that of the reelection of the president. The 1988 Constitution stipulates that the chief executive is allowed one four-year term with no reelection; the same rule applies to state governors and mayors. The Cardoso team in early 1997 proposed an amendment to the constitution to allow for reelection for president and vice president as well as governors and mayors. The proposal moved through a series of required votes during the first quarter of 1997 and is expected to receive final approval by the summer. The amendment appears destined to succeed because of the continuing popularity of the *Real* Plan, the president's popularity in the public opinion polls, and the lack of a credible alternative candidate either within his own coalition or among the opposition. While it is unwise to predict the final judgments of the Brazilian legislature, there appeared to be sufficient momentum in favor of the amendment in mid-1997 to project victory when the final voting takes place. Reelection will allow the president to contemplate a six-year period in which to build coalitions for his reform agenda and to slowly but surely move Brazil in the direction of much needed structural change.

CONCLUSION

Fernando Henrique Cardoso's election in 1994 appeared to herald a new era in Brazil. Cardoso had a popular mandate. He was the author of the most successful economic adjustment program in this century. His cabinet was recognized as talented and task oriented. And the president apparently had put together a loose but majority coalition of party support in the Congress. After a slow start early in 1995, the administration had an important string of victories in mid-1995 with the approval of a set of constitutional amendments to liberalize and modernize the economy.

But since that time, the pace of legislative change has been slow and tortuous. And in mid-1996, the first of a set of phase two reforms was defeated by the very legislative caucuses that were pledged to back the president and his program. What happened? Cardoso overlooked or forgot the traditional basis of Brazilian political life: state and local power brokers who work through putative national political parties to achieve limited benefits and perks for their bases of support. There is little advantage to them to vote in favor of the national interest, since their interest is local and regional. And the president is forced to negotiate and bargain issue by issue, with federal handouts, in a precarious game aimed at winning enough votes to move the reform process forward. But the built-in forces across Brazil that oppose some reform, or some aspects of the reform of some sector, are usually sufficient to stymie specific change. Therefore, it is relatively easy for a deputy to vote for a generic constitutional amendment that has little meaning. But when it comes to implementing legislation that will scale back benefits, reduce the public workforce, cancel subsidies or programs for key constituents, and the like, it is far more difficult to muster a majority—as the social security vote demonstrated in 1996.

But, again, this is not stalemate in the traditional sense. Things do move through the Brazilian Congress but at a pace determined by the interests of the country's principal power brokers. There is always room for compromise, patronage, deals, and bargaining. But the fiscal costs of such a process are high—and ultimately may undo much of the earlier work to restructure the economy. It is understood by the old hands in Brasília and in the states and municipalities that ideology, romanticism, or First World standards are irrelevant. Until there are significant reforms to the electoral system (to probably include some form of district voting), a readjustment of the rules by which parties are organized and registered, and a greater willingness of the Brazilian electorate to hold its elected representatives accountable for their votes, the process of reform will be slow and as much influenced by local considerations as it is—or will be—by the well-intentioned national agenda of reform articulated by the Cardoso government.

NOTES

1. Cardoso was correctly considered to be modern in that his academic background, political experience, and position on the key issues of reform were in sharp contrast to his predecessors, both military and civilian.

2. Ronald M. Schneider, *Brazil: Culture and Politics in a New Industrial Powerhouse* (Boulder: Westview Press, 1996).

3. Barry Ames has written extensively on the electoral system in Brazil; see, for example, "Electoral Strategy Under Open-List Proportional Representation," *American Journal of Political Science*, vol. 39, no. 2 (May 1995).

4. David Fleischer summarizes many aspects of the dynamics of current politics in "Brazilian Politics: Structures, Elections, Parties and Political Groups (1985–1995)," University of Brasília, February 1995 (mimeo).

5. For a recent discussion of the prospects for reform, see

"Prospects for State Reform in Brazil," *Noticias*, Latin American Program, Woodrow Wilson Center, summer 1996.

6. "Adeus as Ilusões, *Jornal do Brasil* (Rio de Janeiro), May 25, 1996, p. 8.

7. "Os Viloes do Real," *Isto É*/1391, May 29, 1996, p. 23.

8. "O Lobby e o Lobo do Homem," *Jornal do Brasil* (Rio de Janeiro), June 2, 1996, p. 3.

9. "Congress Delays Voting," *Gazeta Mercantil,* International Weekly Edition, July 29, 1996, no. 695, p. 2.

2

Is the *Real* Plan for Real?

Albert Fishlow

It has been almost three years since Brazil formally installed its new currency, and not only has it persisted over this entire interval, but it seems capable of continuing. After a series of failed efforts during the decade of the 1980s, starting with the *Cruzado* Plan in February 1986 and including the more radical Collor effort of 1990, Brazil has now apparently crossed the line. The rate of inflation for 1996 was far less than 15 percent, down from 23 percent in 1995. Those are far different from rates that had managed to climb to the thousands of percent by the late 1980s and early 1990s.

Brazil is one of the last countries in the region to succeed in the fight against inflation. Argentina, Bolivia, Chile, Peru, and even Mexico preceded it. Despite the Mexican shock of late 1994, which led to renewed, but temporary, increases in prices with major devaluation, Mexico is now back on the track of significant reduction in the rate; and the much closer trade ties resulting from NAFTA (North American Free Trade Agreement) promise renewed convergence with the lower U.S. level over the future.

For years, there had been a debate in Latin America between monetarists and structuralists concerning macroeconomic policy in the region. Monetarists had insisted that money supply was the key determinant of inflation; government expenditure and deficits simply had to be limited. Structuralists had looked for other factors as ultimately responsible: low supply response, particularly in agriculture; sectoral imbalances; and limited export demand, for example. They were willing to accept some inflation as a trade-off for growth, particularly when government could have access to the inflation tax. Both views had some merit, but only when inflation rates were about 30 percent a year or less. When annual inflation reached four digits, and even greater, there was little doubt that one had to start anew. That issue has now been decided, and new currency regimes have been installed almost everywhere in the region—ironically by the left rather than the right. The failure of the many military regimes in the 1970s and early 1980s to adjust to the debt crisis created a unique opportunity for the new civilian governments replacing them.

This recent Brazilian success in controlling inflation has not, however, come cheaply. Brazil's rate of growth has dipped from close to 6 percent in 1994 to a level of some 3 percent in 1996, which is far below the twentieth-century trend. Monetary policy has been tight; only now are real interest rates falling to levels of some 20 percent a year, after having been much higher early on. Debt has rapidly expanded, particularly debt held internally. The balance of payments has swung from significant surplus into deficit, and there have been fears that the impressive movement toward liberalization of trade and receptivity of foreign capital may now be halted. Foreign reserves have hit record levels of near $60 billion, but with a consequent cost. Brazil is forced to reward investors with much higher returns than it itself can earn by buying U.S. government securities.

Some observers have responded to this difficult situation negatively. Rudiger Dornbusch, a highly regarded international economist, explicitly called for more competitive exchange rates and lower interest rates in June 1996, warning that the Mexican disequilibrium provided relevant precedent for eventual Brazilian failure: "Brazilian policymakers, basking in the admiration of the press and the public, misread their situation. They underestimate the internationalization of their economy and their dependence on external capital. Either the government starts reform with big and eager steps, or they should expect major trouble. There won't be an exact replay of Mexico, but even half that experience would be a dramatic setback."[1] Others in Brazil have been especially critical of the high-interest policy that has contributed to slowing performance, and still others of the relative lack of attention paid to the substantial inequality of income. Dealing seriously with stabilization is a novelty in Brazilian experience. It seems extraordinary that the attempt has been as successful as it has.

The net reaction of Brazilian voters to the changes in economic policy has been sufficiently positive in the 1996 municipal elections, despite the government's defeat in São Paulo, to encourage
Fernando Henrique Cardoso to pursue a constitutional change
permitting his reelection. This endorsement extends the first positive response, in the presidential, state, and congressional elections of 1994, to the *Real* Plan. Cardoso was then elected in the
first round, defeating his leading opponent, Lula, head of the
Labor Party. Now, bolstered by broad victories, especially in
smaller localities, he seeks to ensure the continuity of the structural changes that have been introduced.

Here is a three-part interim assessment of what has been done
so far. First, there is a review of the internal policies the Brazilian
government has followed in recent years. Major attention is
directed to the fiscal deficit. Several years ago, I pointed to fiscal
inadequacy as being central to the inflation problem in the region
and argued against being able to quickly persuade citizens that
inflation was over: "Rational expectations theory has been a mis-
leading guide in its implication that inflation can be stopped at
modest costs, something all too appealing to Latin American ears.
There has been too much attention to changing expectations and
establishing the credibility of fixed exchange rates and monetary
restraint and too little to the need to remedy the underlying fiscal
imbalance."[2] There seems little reason to change that assessment
now.

Second, the external accounts are examined. Imports have
played a critical role during the success of the last two years in
checking domestic price rises. And the relative stabilizing, indeed
strengthening, of the exchange rate served as an important device
to signal the government's commitment to maintain the *real*'s
value. But the balance of payments has now moved into deficit on
merchandise account. Is such a shift an indication of basic trouble
ahead? Should there be more concern with the early appreciation
of the *real* and a readiness to accept greater devaluation, even if
that were to spark more rapid inflation?

Third is the somewhat disappointing picture of fundamental
economic reforms adopted by Congress in the first years of the
Cardoso government. It has proven almost impossible to obtain
the 60 percent affirmative vote required to amend the constitution. Tax reform has not proceeded. Revision of the social security
system has been disappointingly minimal. Administrative reform,
designed to cut back on the number of government employees, is

still under discussion. Privatization has moved very slowly, despite early passage of an amendment ending the monopoly position of Petrobrás. Will such performance mean eventual failure for the government? Or were the initial expectations of the new Cardoso government excessive?

DOMESTIC REFORM

Brazilian economic policy changed decisively in 1979 with the reemergence of Antonio Delfim Neto as minister of finance. Up to that point, despite the 1973 oil crisis and a subsequent slowing of domestic growth from the days of the "economic miracle," (1968–1973), policy had remained committed to rates of inflation no greater than 40–50 percent a year, even if it meant slower real expansion. Yet it was still an era of growth: the average rate of expansion remained at about 5 percent from 1974 through 1979. Delfim promised faster growth and, partially in response to increasing labor strikes, a better income distribution. Neither objective materialized. Higher inflation, the second oil price increase, and a lesser Brazilian access to external lending facilities were among the problems soon encountered. Brazil was forced into a continuing, but unfulfilled, arrangement with the International Monetary Fund. A number of agreements were concluded, but none were really implemented. Deficits were not eliminated. The debt shock was larger than had earlier been appreciated.

Delfim's special blend of heterodoxy, whereby he was going to restore rapid Brazilian growth, failed in 1979–1980 for four reasons.[3] First, it suffered from a large dose of excess demand; unlike the "miracle" years, there was no elastic domestic supply available to respond to greater pressures on the demand side. A second problem was the effort to better the income distribution through more frequent wage adjustments. In November 1979, when inflation already was creeping up to well over 50 percent annually, the wage system was changed from adjustment once a year to twice, thereby ensuring less erosion from unadjusted interim inflation. It was not that the law contributed to higher inflation but rather that, by making adjustment even more frequently dependent upon *past* trends, it inhibited any significant deceleration in inflation without a large real wage increase. Third, imports were unavailable to serve as a means of satisfying domestic demand

and disciplining price setting; Brazil was in the midst of a second oil crisis. And finally, this was hardly the moment when a simple reversal of inflationary expectations was feasible. The commitment to expansionary domestic policies completely negated the logic of prefixed monetary correction and exchange rate devaluation that guided policy.

As the economic situation deteriorated, with inflation exceeding 300 percent annually and per capita income growth approximating zero, the military government finally conceded defeat just before the 1984 election. It had failed at what it was supposed to deal with best: reality in the face of adversity. The new civilian president, Tancredo Neves, elected indirectly, died unexpectedly shortly before his inauguration in March 1985; in his place came the vice president–elect, José Sarney. His ability to manage proved deceptive.

In early 1986 came the first of several Brazilian efforts to shut down inflation: the *Cruzado* Plan, under the aegis of Dilson Funaro, the minister of finance. Although it came later than its Argentine predecessor, it had similar intellectual origins and in the end mimicked many of the characteristics of the *Austral* Plan.

Wages were readjusted, depending upon their date of negotiation, to approximate a consistent real value independent of contract date. That meant increases for those workers with months to go before their automatic adjustment, and reductions for those who had just received their increase. Wages, prices, and the exchange rate were then frozen. Indexation, earlier central to maintaining inertial inflation intact by simply duplicating in the present what had happened in the past, was virtually eliminated. An allowance for adjusting wages was guaranteed for increases over 20 percent a year, a concession to the laboring class that was soon to prove costly. The economy was remonetized to avoid the deflationary effects of a high interest rate, such as was seen in the Argentine *Austral* Plan. This increase in the money supply was initially met by increases in demand for monetary balances, and the economy featured high rates of real growth with stable (because they were fixed) prices.

While these measures were received with initial enthusiasm and success—the monthly rate of inflation initially fell to negligible amounts and Sarney's popularity soared—the end result was not a happy one. Here, as in their initial preparation, *Austral* and *Cruzado* shared a common fate. Their failure was due to excessively expansive wage, monetary, and fiscal policies. There were too many green lights. Wages increased too rapidly owing to the plan's provision for a 15 percent bonus for those receiving only a minimum salary, and 8 percent for the rest. In addition, the consumer boom in 1986 provoked labor shortages and even further increases in wages. On the monetary side, it is clear that the government took full advantage of the increased demand for money, and then some; real interest rates turned positive initially but then retreated. And the operational fiscal balance, adjusting for inflation instead of going to zero as had initially been projected, amounted to a deficit of 3.6 percent of GDP. And this ignores some of the increased expenditures actually made during 1986, in part because of the fall elections, and not paid until the following year.

Under these circumstances, it was only a question of time before the plan would come to an end. There was a partial reform in November, after the elections, but it was a case of too little too late. The government was implicitly trying to reenact the 1964 program of real wage cuts to restore fiscal stability as well as to equilibrate the balance of payments. But the constraints of democracy put limits on the exercise. No one was willing to concede his or her real income so that the income of others might eventually rise. Brazil had come close, but failed.

Despite a subsequent effort, such as the Bresser Plan in 1987, which temporarily worked but did not find a president willing to accept the higher taxes that were essential to success, inflation soared and real growth faltered. By the month before the inauguration of Sarney's successor, Fernando Collor, in anticipation of a new effort to stem the tide, the increase in prices had reached the extraordinary level of about 90 percent. That translates to an annual rate that begins to look like hyperinflation of the historical German variety.

Not surprisingly, an anti-inflation effort was undertaken by the new government immediately upon its inauguration. This plan was apparently bolder than earlier efforts. All but modest bank deposits were frozen, as were wages and prices, and economic activity immediately reacted adversely. But evasions of restrictions soon occurred, additional reforms did not take place, the price restrictions were released, and inflation was back—this time at a much higher annual rate, supported by an expanding monetary supply. Collor II was a feeble effort by the same team to regain control of the inflationary process; its major effort was to recognize that if a tight fiscal policy were to be sustained, prices of public goods that had been held constant would have to be raised.

In a matter of months, the Ministry of Finance then changed hands from Zélia Cardoso de Mello to Marcílio Marques Moreira. With that transfer came a change in policy: now the effort was concentrated on getting the fundamentals right. That revision only had the effect of immediately raising the monthly rate of increase from 10 to 20 percent. The market correctly anticipated that a longer and harder battle against inflation had to be fought. Collor's impeachment in September 1992 for misuse of private funds during his presidential campaign put a stop to any possibility for innovative policy. Interest turned passionately to politics. Collor lost.

As a result, at the end of 1992, Itamar Franco, another vice president, formally assumed the presidency. After promising priority to ending inflation, but not really appreciating how, and four finance ministers later, Itamar finally appointed Fernando Henrique Cardoso as finance minister in June 1993. The *Real* Plan was the eventual consequence, coming into formal effect on July 1, 1994, although some of the steps had been gradually introduced since the beginning of Cardoso's tenure.

That strategy emerged from virtually the same set of economists that had been active in the initial formulation of the *Cruzado* Plan: Persio Arida, Edmar Bacha, Andre Lara Resende, and Gustavo Franco were the central figures. Nor was the plan startlingly different. This time, however, there were no wage and price controls, nor any commitment to an indexation mechanism that would come back to haunt their efforts. Such a policy was possible only because earlier efforts had failed. And provision to ensure a large *immediate* increase in imports ensured that the forces of the market would be used immediately to reinforce the effort.

The *Real* Plan can be seen as a play in three acts. The first act, given great weight, was devoted to fiscal adjustment. A balanced budget for 1994 was prepared and actually passed by Congress. It was clearly understood that absent such approval, nothing would follow. That helped to focus legislative attention. In the second act, in March 1994, a new monetary unit was created, the *unidade real de valor,* or URV; at the same time, the old *cruzeiro* remained as currency and continued to circulate. Price changes occurred in the latter at a rate of 40 percent and more per month, but not in the former. All prices therefore eventually became dual. This time the market was used as a mechanism for the monetary conversion rather than the obligatory fixing of wages and prices. The third act was the translation of the URV into the new currency, the *real,* on July 1, 1994. Expected to exchange with the dollar at a one to one ratio, there occurred instead a rapid appreciation of the *real* in the first months as domestic prices rose but the exchange rate, supported by substantial reserves, did not change. With the substantial pressure caused by the devaluation of the Mexican *peso* in December 1994, Brazil was forced to continue to follow a fixed exchange rate longer than it wished in order to achieve credibility. This led to somewhat greater appreciation than successful plans originally show.

After nearly three years, the *Real* Plan stands clearly as Brazil's most successful effort at stabilization. The critical question now is its permanence, which depends fundamentally on the credibility of governmental fiscal policy. Through the present, confidence in the *real* has been created primarily by tight monetary policy and a virtual exchange rate anchor, as we explore more fully in the next section. This has led to high real rates of interest, which have declined somewhat in the second half of 1996, as well as to overvaluation. Both of these prices must relinquish their central roles in the future if growth is to occur at an acceptable rate and equity is to receive the attention it merits.

The needed medium-term alternative is tighter, continuous control over the fiscal deficit. This is essential, moreover, if government savings are to play a major role, as they should and indeed must, in financing private investment. What makes the fiscal situation even more crucial is the substantial attention it has recently received in Europe and the United States. In both these developed parts of the world, it has become the centerpiece of economic policy. President Clinton stressed his ability to eliminate the deficit as a central part of his successful reelection campaign. Throughout the European Union, as the magic hour of currency unification approaches in 1999, both right and left are strongly committed to reductions in the deficit as the only way of ensuring future low rates of inflation.

In Brazil, this issue is central. The Banco de Investimentos Garantia recently reported: "Brazil's unrelenting problem is to achieve a fiscal stance compatible with the maintenance of economic stability. Concern on this point is exacerbated by frequent announcement of measures to bail out individual sectors, of securitization of existing debt, and of weighty expenditure plans—as well as by a timid attitude to cuts in spending and implementation of the privatization program."[4] Table 2.1 provides the underlying data back to 1985 for both the primary and operational deficits; the former excludes interest paid on government securities, while the latter includes real interest expenditures.

Table 2.1 Public Sector Deficit[a] (percentage of GDP)

	Primary	Operational[b]
1985	−2.6	4.4
1986	−1.6	3.6
1987	1.0	5.7
1988	−0.9	4.8
1989	1.0	6.9
1990	−4.6	−1.3
1991	−2.7	0.2
1992	−2.6	2.6
1993	−1.8	0.7
1994	−5.2	−1.3
1995	−0.4	5.0
1996	−0.1	3.9

Source: Central Bank of Brazil, *Brazil Economic Program*, 1996.
Notes: a. Includes state-owned corporations; negative values indicate surplus
b. Includes interest payments on public debt

This information is central to any analysis of the Brazilian economy in the last ten years. It helps to explain the failure of the *Cruzado* Plan, as the primary deficit actually increased in 1986 relative to 1985; it indicates the basis of Bresser Pereira's resignation in December 1987, as little effort was made to deal with the need to increase revenues; it reveals the major effort made during the initial Collor period not only to reduce outlays, but also to cut back interest expenditures through cancellation of part of the domestic debt—a strategy that did not last. And it clearly shows the consequence of the very successful attempt in 1994, with the introduction of the *real*, to increase revenues and reduce expenditures. As can be seen, the primary surplus attained in that year was the largest on record, as was the operational result.

The soaring deficit in 1995 is clearly evident, the result not of inadequate revenues—they reached a high of 31 percent of product in that year—but of a sharp increase in expenditures. That result owed itself primarily to rises in outlays of the federal government and of the Central Bank. Personnel costs entered as a major factor, due to the inflation-indexed rise in salaries in January 1995. The consequence was a large rise in net domestic debt in this period to finance the deficit; it went from 20 percent of GDP to 26 percent.

Despite this situation, the rate of inflation continued to fall through 1995 and 1996, and real interest rates have declined significantly as well. One important reason that stabilization has remained credible is found, ironically, in the modest growth performance of the Brazilian economy: after reaching 5.9 percent in 1994 and slowing a bit to 4.2 percent in 1995, it has been reduced further to less than 3 percent in 1996. In 1997, only modest acceleration is foreseen. Rarely has policy been so consistently and effectively applied in Brazilian experience. But high interest rates and limited real investment do not translate into permanent solutions.

The real test comes in the deficit figures for 1996 and 1997. Earlier government estimates of a reduction from 5 to 2.5 percent of GDP in 1996 were clearly exaggerated. What will count to reinforce stabilization and allow the economy to resume growth is evidence that the deficit was lower in 1996 than the previous year and indications that it will fall further in 1997. The first part has been achieved. Surpluses for the second half of 1996 have reduced the negative numbers of the first half, which actually exceeded those of 1995. Even more important, in 1997, a series of changes can be anticipated whose total effect should be significant.

First, somewhat more rapid growth of the economy will lead to more public revenue; second, declining domestic interest rates, which should stabilize in 1997, will reduce the cost of servicing the internal debt; third, changes in the social security system should permit a surplus rather than the recurrent deficit to occur; and, fourth, public sector wage costs are predicted to be relatively smaller than they had been. All these factors exclude still another: the effect of privatization of Vale do Rio Doce as well as the opening of the telecommunications sector and others to private entry.

This combination should lead to important consolidation of the gains so far achieved. Brazil will have given evidence not only of stabilization but, even more, of an ability to react effectively to the threat posed by short-term reversal to the government balance. That is exactly what occurred in the case of Chile during the presidency of Patricio Aylwin, 1989–1994. In 1990, the ability of

the government to reduce growth, and thus to counter inflationary pressures, was decisive in showing that democracy did not
translate into ineffective economic policy. Such a comparison
augurs well for Brazil's economic as well as political future.

EXTERNAL ACCOUNTS

Brazil began the *Real* Plan with a commitment to exchange rate
fixity as an anchor for the new price level. In that fashion, uncertainty as to future movements of domestic prices is restrained.
One of the immediate, not wholly expected consequences was significant appreciation of the *real:* it quickly went from its anticipated value of one to one with the dollar to something like $1.15
within a matter of three months. Such appreciation helped control
inflation by making imports, in rapidly increasing quantities,
much more competitive with domestic products. Imports quickly
rose from $33 billion in 1994 to close to $50 billion in 1995. Indeed,
this reliance upon direct competition of foreign products was a
fundamental difference from the earlier *Cruzado* Plan, when
imports expanded too late.

Brazil, in part pressured by a progressively less favorable balance of payments and in part forced to delay regular devaluation
by reason of the "tequila effect" derivative from the Mexican
exchange crisis in December 1994, moved to a variable exchange
rate, within a defined band, in April 1995.[5] Since that time, the *real*
has kept approximate pace with the difference between internal
price inflation in Brazil and that in the United States.

A major question has arisen as to the consequences of such a
period of extensive appreciation. On the one side, as cited earlier,
some economists are calling for more rapid devaluation to stimu-
late exports; their logic is supported by empirical studies that
show that appreciation beyond a certain point is almost certainly
followed by eventual devaluation. Others are persuaded that the
policy currently being pursued is the correct one; they rely on
continuing productivity change as an element moving the rate
progressively closer to equilibrium.

Note that any commitment to Argentine-like fixed convertibility, in order to sustain a permanent anchor to prices, quickly
lost support in the Brazilian case. That solution places too much
weight on response of capital inflow to domestic interest rate sig-
nals to find broad acceptability in a large country. Argentina

could go back to the gold standard, which it had followed off and on since the last quarter of the nineteenth century. In Brazil, convertibility was a temporary expedient in the first decade of the twentieth century.

Several considerations are relevant to deciding whether Brazil has decisively erred. First comes the claim that appreciation of the *real* has attained more than 50 percent since its 1994 introduction. That result is dependent, however, on using the Brazilian consumer price index as the relevant price measure. But the consumer price index includes a high proportion of nontradable services that do not enter into international exchange, such as housing, health services, and education outlays. If one substitutes the wholesale price index as a deflator, much better at measuring the price of goods exclusively, the conclusion is substantially altered. One then finds that real appreciation has been equivalent to a little more than 10 percent; such a comparison disregards the relative productivity advances resulting from rationalization of production within Brazil owing to greater trade. The difference between the two price indexes increases substantially over time; it is less than 10 percent in the fall of 1994 and around 30 percent in recent months, correlated with the rise in imports.

It is obviously difficult to come up with a single number. There is no doubt some overvaluation, as is characteristic of all stabilization efforts from initially high inflation. But most analysts currently assess it at about 15 percent rather than 50. That brings the *Real* Plan within the margin of probable success rather than undoubted failure.

We can examine this matter with greater precision. Table 2.2 records measures of real exchange rates in the year previous to a successful stabilization program as well as in the two subsequent years. Four additional Latin American countries are included: Argentina, Bolivia, Mexico, and Peru; Israel is shown as well. I use both consumer and wholesale prices, where available, to indicate the divergence between the measures. Real exchange rate indexes based on consumer prices tend to change relatively more, everywhere, simply because of the greater role of services in the index.

There is a clear initial period during which the stable exchange rate becomes overvalued as domestic prices, particularly of nontradables, rise relatively more quickly.[6] That is what using the exchange rate as an anchor entails. But note that already in the second year of the stabilization program, there is a

Table 2.2 Real Exchange Rates

	Year before stabilization	Two years after stabilization	
Argentina			
	1990	1992	1993
Based on:			
Wholesale price index	100	91.1	90.3
Consumer price index	100	59.9	54.6
Real efficient exchange rate index for exports	100	77.5	74.4
Bolivia			
	1985	1987	1988
Based on:			
Consumer price index	100	108.2	106.7
Real efficient exchange rate index for exports	100	165.0	175.2
Peru			
	1989	1991	1992
Based on:			
Consumer price index	100	74.0	68.9
Real efficient exchange rate index for exports	100	67.2	66.3
Israel			
	1984	1986	1987
Based on:			
Consumer price index	100	84.7	75.8
Mexico			
	1987	1989	1990
Based on:			
Wholesale price index	100	74.0	68.6
Consumer price index	100	69.4	62.7
Real efficient exchange rate index for exports	100	76.3	74.0
Brazil			
	1993	1995	1996[a]
Based on:			
Wholesale price index	100	75.5	74.8
Consumer price index	100	56.2	53.2
Real efficient exchange rate index for exports	100	61.7	58.4

Sources: International Monetary Fund, *International Financial Statistics Yearbook.* For real effective exchange rate indexes for exports, ECLAC, *Notas Sobre la Economía y el Desarrollo,* 1995.
Note: a. Estimate using a 15% year-on-year change in consumer prices and 10% in wholesale prices

tendency for greater convergence to occur. The real moral of the story is that adequate external reserves are necessary to sustain an anti-inflation program during its first phase. But thereafter, internal productivity change at higher rates, the ultimate objective of any stabilization effort, can begin to erode the initial price difference and lead to greater competitiveness.

Second, Brazil has maintained a much higher level of reserves than has been characteristic of other countries. Reserves are just about $60 billion in the fall of 1996, or about fifteen months of import coverage. And they are costly: given the differences between internal and external interest rates, the annual charge to Brazil is somewhere in the vicinity of $5–6 billion. One of the great difficulties is that because they represent short-term holdings, reserve levels can fluctuate considerably depending upon external evaluation of risk. In early 1995, after the Mexican crisis, Brazil's holdings of reserves dropped sharply, only to recover later in the year. The change was of the order of $20 billion; lesser reserves could have meant a liquidity crisis.

Such holdings provide assurance against external shocks that might otherwise have a much greater impact. Contrast the decline in Argentine GDP in 1995 in excess of 4 percent with the continuing income rise in Brazil. These reserves also are likely to cost less in the future, as domestic real interest rates continue to fall. Note as well that larger foreign direct investment is beginning to occur. Brazil has received more than $9 billion in this form in 1996, well up from the levels barely over a billion dollars just a few years ago. A strategy that maintains reserve levels but does not seek to enlarge them is a feasible one in circumstances where foreign investors begin to concern themselves with the longer-term future of the country rather than immediate interest rate differentials. That hopefully is the situation Brazil is beginning to enter.

A third observation relates to a need for continuing export growth. Here is where overvaluation exacts its negative impact by making Brazilian products more expensive. New provisions were enacted in the fall of 1996 eliminating the state tax that previously prevailed on exports, seeking to reduce the "Brazil cost." Few expressions give a greater sense of the enhanced consciousness of relative competitiveness than this one. A different view with regard to foreign trade and its importance to the country is now emerging. Historically in Brazil, beyond the major primary goods sold abroad, the export market was primarily viewed as a residual, and growing internal demand for industrial products was always preferential to reliance on sales overseas. With the reduction in import duties and the additional competitiveness this introduces into the system, exports equally are benefited.

There is another potential market of interest that should not be ignored. MERCOSUR suddenly has become a market of interest and one whose continuing growth can provide great opportunity, especially with the addition of Chile and Bolivia as associates in June 1996 and Venezuela likely to come in before long. Moreover, the fact of an Argentine fixed rate and extensive trade between the two countries imposes greater discipline upon Brazil than had occurred earlier.

One need not anticipate that Brazilian export proportions will radically increase following the Asian model. Asian countries have been able to achieve, and sustain for relatively long periods, much higher rates of export than domestic growth. Brazil has too large and varied a domestic market for that form of export-led expansion. But export-adequate development, allowing an annual real enlargement in exports of the order of 1–2 percent greater than product growth, is a style that makes eminent sense. For too long, the domestic market has been the most important priority in Brazilian objectives. But international trade growth over the last thirty years has been at a rate twice that of domestic increase. Brazil has approximately conformed to that rule over the period since 1980, but only because product growth was so limited. It now remains to be seen whether an emphasis on external sales will survive a resumption in internal Brazilian growth. If it does not, the ability to sustain low rates of inflation will come into question.

Fourth, a fundamental reason Brazil is not in danger of repeating the unfortunate Mexican denouement of 1994 is that its dependence on foreign capital inflows is much smaller. The current account deficit is some 3 percent of product rather than the 8+ percent achieved by Mexico in 1994. It is unlikely, and indeed unwise, to expand such reliance on external savings in the future. But that implies the need to develop domestic sources of saving necessary to achieve a growth rate of between 5 and 6 percent on a regular basis. Something more than 22 percent of product, plus 3 percent from abroad, will have to be given over to domestic saving, contrasted to a figure of perhaps 17–18 percent currently. That real requirement cannot be ignored.

All four of these points suggest that Brazil is within reach of a coherent and consistent external policy that can be sustained over time. It is obvious from what has happened in Mexico that external balance is as necessary as internal equilibrium for continuous growth to occur. That reality has sunk in. What is essential is that it not be easily forgotten.

THE PROCESS OF ECONOMIC REFORM

Brazil frequently receives negative or barely passing marks for the reforms it has accomplished since the election of Fernando Henrique Cardoso as president. He started his term boldly, passing an array of constitutional reforms that included ending the monopoly of the state oil company, Petrobrás. He programmed other needed reforms—in the areas of taxation, employee rights, social security, and others. Thus far, however, despite extensive congressional discussion, he seems to have been unable to gain passage of these reforms, at least not in their original form. And many of the strictly economic measures initially conceived, dealing with taxation and distribution of revenues to states and localities, have been put aside.

Indeed, the strategy seems to have fundamentally changed. Instead of a single four-year term, Cardoso has now obtained an amendment that will permit reelection; with that longer term in mind, he has taken a more gradual approach to the array of reforms required. No longer is the image that of President Roosevelt and the New Deal. It has become more like that of President Clinton and his liberal conservatism.

Such a change makes good sense in the present Brazilian context. It is difficult to imagine, especially within a democratic regime, an ability to achieve the changes Brazil requires within a single-term presidency. It is no accident that Argentina and Peru reelected Presidents Menem and Fujimori after they began far-reaching alterations within their countries. These matters take time if they are to prove permanent. And they also eventually require alternation of political parties to validate their continuity.

It is easy, within such a climate, to underestimate the significant modifications already accomplished in Brazil. First and foremost is the continuing success of the *Real* Plan. Second is a prospective set of internal changes that would reduce the historic role of government as the principal prominent economic actor. Privatization is very much on the way in 1997; an example at the national level involves CVRD, one of the largest and consistently profitable mining enterprises in Latin America. Other state enterprises, primarily utilities, are coming along as part of the restructuring of state governments and banks that has clearly begun. Brazil was fortunate in not having to suffer a generalized financial crisis to begin the process of reform. Telecommunications were recently opened in the cellular area, and others will follow.

Third, important reforms have occurred in primary and secondary education. Changes under way in curriculum will reduce substantially the repetition level in the public schools. Over time, such modifications will prove fundamental. Fourth, changes in the social security system, while still not complete, will enable some fiscal relief over the short term and provide greater latitude for increased public savings at the national level.

The initial results in the municipal elections extend such optimism to the political level. While the PSDB, Cardoso's party, has lost São Paulo, as well as Rio and Belo Horizonte, it has done quite well in smaller localities. There is widespread sentiment that this election was based on local rather than national conditions. Economic growth is reviving, prices continue stable, the balance of payments may equilibrate, and reform is slowly occurring. In these circumstances, a second wave of energy is likely in adopting the constitutional changes required to push forward the economy.

As of mid-1997, Cardoso is the favorite in the 1998 presidential election. The real question is the cost: Can the requisite electioneering be carried out without impeding efforts to reduce the deficit and to further open the economy?

Prospects at this writing are promising. Brazil is moving into the new century under more favorable economic and political conditions than it has experienced for several decades. For one thing, it is confronting economic reality in a responsible fashion. For another, the wealth of individual parties, which has so influenced Brazilian political evolution, is likely to be reduced. Localism and regionalism seem ready to give way to more national, but not nationalistic, sentiments.

CONCLUSION

Brazil has begun to catch up to the rest of the continent in terms of economic reform. Brazilians have not replicated a new "economic miracle" of rapid expansion such as occurred at the end of the 1960s. This time, the reconstruction is more fundamental and directed toward the long term. This time, the changes are being widely discussed and debated rather than being imposed arbitrarily. This time, success is measured by slow continuous rises in income rather than meteoric and immediate gains. And this time, the basic theme in Brazilian development is much more outward-oriented than at virtually any time since the 1920s.

As it moves in this direction, Brazil is also beginning to exert the inevitable power associated with its size. As noted earlier, MERCOSUR has already expanded its membership and is now considering affiliation with the European Union and not merely the extension of NAFTA. As the largest member country and the one with the most diversified trade in composition and direction, Brazil is at the center of such negotiations. President Cardoso has made a record number of trips abroad as Brazilian foreign relations are enlivened and become more sophisticated. Brazil's goal of membership on the Security Council of the United Nations is much more likely to be satisfied by outstanding economic performance than by economic difficulties.

But one must remain cautious. Latin America has not yet definitively emerged from its difficult depression of the 1980s, one that has proven far deeper and longer than the Great Depression. Confidence has gradually increased throughout the region but could quickly turn to disenchantment again. An important factor going for Brazilian economic success is that virtually every other Latin American country is proceeding in very similar fashion. This commonality of problems, and of potential solutions, helps provide optimism in the specific case of Brazil. So too does the strong political commitment to sustain current policies rather than opt for immediate higher growth with inevitable accelerating inflation rates. Creditworthiness of recent origin is easily lost.

When one considers all sides of the issue, it is difficult to arrive at a negative judgment. Brazil and the region as a whole have decisively changed. One can venture the guess that the *Real* Plan is very likely to be for real.

NOTES

1. "Economic Viewpoint," *Business Week,* June 10, 1996, p. 24.
2. "The Latin American State," *Journal of Economic Perspectives,* vol. 4, no. 3 (1990): 69.

3. For fuller treatment, see my "A Tale of Two Presidents: The Political Economy of Crisis Management," in Alfred Stepan, ed., *Democratizing Brazil* (New York: Oxford University Press, 1989), pp. 83–119.

4. Banco de Investimentos Garantia, *Brazil Research: Macroeconomic Outlook,* August 30, 1996.

5. Brazil was forced to wait, lest international speculation quickly amplify intended small changes into a very large devaluation that would have meant the end of the *Real* Plan.

6. The one apparent exception here is Bolivia. But different data from the IMF confirm a very large change in the value of its calculated real effective exchange rate in 1985.

3

Redressing Inequalities: Brazil's Social Agenda at Century's End

Amaury de Souza

It has taken more than a decade of sluggish growth and raging inflation to move the issue of poverty to the front burner of public debate in Brazil and to shake the Brazilians' age-old indifference toward the poor. Much of this new awareness has sprung from two not altogether unrelated facts. One is the increased visibility of the poor, who are jammed in sprawling urban squatter settlements scarred by joblessness, drug abuse, and crime. The other is the realization that the steep inequalities in the distribution of schooling and income in Brazil could make the country a loser in the global race for jobs and capital.

Poverty became more visible as the rural poor streamed by the millions into the coastal cities of the southeast, where the more affluent Brazilians could see them. In the past, poverty was largely a rural problem. As late as the mid-1970s, most families below the poverty line still lived in the countryside. Today the poor are almost equally divided between the rural areas of the impoverished northeast and the mushrooming squatter settlements that ring the main cities of the prosperous southeast.

Although these alarming trends are not new, the fear they inspire is. Poverty and social uprooting have fractured families, sending hordes of children into the streets to survive by their wits alone. An urban underclass has emerged, and with it has come drug addiction and crime. The changing nature of poverty inevitably changed the way in which the poor are seen. The image of the favela dweller, enduring year-round hardship to be able to savor one night at the Carnival parade, has been replaced in the public eye by the no less stereotypical AK-47 automatic rifle–toting favela drug lord.

What started as a vague presentiment that things were taking a turn for the worse blossomed in the early 1990s into a premonition of impending social disaster. Surveys conducted in both houses of Congress in November 1991 and March 1995 by the Institute of Economic, Social, and Political Studies of São Paulo (IDESP) found that a vast majority of senators and federal deputies feared for the future of Brazil in the face of persistent poverty and social inequality (see Table 3.1).[1]

Table 3.1   Congressional Assessment of Risks Associated with the Persistence of Poverty and Inequality (percent "certain" or "quite probable")

Risks	November 1991	March 1995
A chronic state of social unrest	40	35
An unviable market economy	30	28
A takeover by an extremist movement	11	6
A return to power by the military	9	9
Secession of states from the nation	8	9
No opinion/other answers	2	13
Total respondents	(406)	(484)

Sources: Bolívar Lamounier and Amaury de Souza, *O Congresso Nacional e a Crise Brasileira*, São Paulo: IDESP, November 1991; and *O Congresso Nacional e as Reformas*, São Paulo: IDESP, March 1995.
Note: The question was: "If Brazil does not substantially reduce poverty and social and regional inequalities within ten years, how likely is it to face the following risks?"

Although the legislators were interviewed three years apart and in two different terms of Congress, more than a third in both instances agreed that if Brazil did not "substantially reduce poverty and social and regional inequalities within the next ten years," it would face a chronic state of social unrest. Nearly a third thought that under such circumstances Brazil could not sustain a free market economy. Close to 10 percent predicted an extremist takeover of some sort, the return of the military to power, or the secession of states from the country.

It may be argued that it is the crime epidemic rather than the fear of civil convulsion that has been fueling the sense of urgency so evident in Congress. However, no matter how remote it may be, the probability of violent collective disturbance remains a cause for concern among large segments of the public. In the past few years, the Landless Rural Workers Movement (Movimento dos Trabalhadores Rurais Sem Terra—MST) has orchestrated the invasion of several farms that fit the profile for acquisition or expropriation by the government under its land reform program. Although such invasions have usually been conducted peacefully, the MST's confrontational strategy has produced a deep sense of unease, especially after clashes with the police left scores of demonstrators dead in Corumbiara and Eldorado dos Carajás.

On the other hand, most legislators would probably agree that if discontent does turn into open conflict, it will most likely be contained within narrow confines. Reflecting on similar results from a previous elite survey conducted by IDESP in late 1989 and early 1990, then Senator Fernando Henrique Cardoso (currently president of Brazil) pointed out the pitfalls of believing that civil convulsion threatened a breakdown of order: "The reality is that Brazil is nowadays a complex and highly segmented society. Social unrest in one sector does not necessarily spread to the next. It is not a general process, with repercussions capable of crippling the system as a whole."[2]

What does seem to frighten Brazilian elites in and out of Congress is the real possibility that the country may not live up to its emerging market potential. Two characteristics of Brazil's economy raise doubts as to its capacity to adjust rapidly to a less regulated marketplace and increased international competition. The first one is great inequalities in schooling. About half of Brazil's labor force either has no formal schooling or did not complete primary school, and only 37 percent of the population ages sixteen to eighteen is enrolled in secondary schools. Despite the rapid expansion of the education system since the late 1970s, many fear that low levels of education may seriously jeopardize Brazil's future growth. The other cause for concern is the rigid and segmented arrangements in the labor market. An entrenched institutional setting discourages the creation of the better-paid, higher-quality jobs that are needed to increase the long-term productivity of the work force. Highly segmented labor markets, in which a vast informal sector coexists with a modern industrial economy, are particularly vulnerable to changing market conditions. If only a few are able to take advantage of emerging economic opportunities, growth is likely to widen, rather than narrow, inequalities in employment and income.

With the awareness of sprawling poverty and declining life opportunities came the realization among the elites and the public alike that government was a large part of the problem. Cutbacks in spending on health care and family welfare in the early 1990s left the poor to fend for themselves. As the social safety net frayed, the public came to doubt whether the government could really solve Brazil's social and economic difficulties. Public outrage was compounded by the perception that government was not only inept but that corruption and profligacy reigned in high office. Abuse of power and privilege in the Collor administration sent millions of Brazilians pouring into the streets to demand the president's impeachment.

It may be too soon to write off the appeal of populist solutions, but public discontent with government mismanagement and waste appears to have set the stage for new approaches to dealing with Brazil's social agenda. This mood was reflected in Cardoso's striking victory at the polls in 1994. In forging a viable coalition between social democrats and liberals, Cardoso made it clear that redressing inequalities will remain only a lofty ideal if reforms that open the way for a sustainable market-oriented economy are not effected. This extraordinary consensus represents a great opportunity for reform. The challenge for the Cardoso administration is to turn opportunity into reality.

SOCIAL POLICY AND GOVERNMENT REGULATION

The institutional features of Brazil's social policy are a legacy of the state-centered growth model that took shape in the aftermath of the 1930 revolution. Centralization and corporatism were the hallmark of the emerging regime. Centralization was rooted in the conviction that new national institutions were needed to modernize the economy and break the hold of state oligarchies. Corporatism, in turn, originated from a consensus regarding the dangers of an unregulated marketplace and the need to protect workers from the economic hardships associated with industrialization. At the core of the model, therefore, was the premise that growth should be promoted by an activist central government and a labor peace obtained in exchange for social protection.[3]

The basic institutions of this corporatist system were a body of labor laws (Consolidation of Labor Laws—CLT), a network of labor courts, and a social security system. From 1930 onward, legal action rather than collective bargaining became the paramount means of regulating industrial relations and disputes. The CLT specified in excruciating detail the rights and obligations of employers and workers. It also established the basic framework for union organization. Institutional power, in the form of grants of authority, has been a crucial component of union power ever since unions were granted exclusive rights of representation over whole categories of labor as well as the power to levy compulsory dues on workers, even unaffiliated ones. Guaranteed financing and protection from competition within their jurisdictions meant that unions became increasingly unwilling to challenge the status quo. As a result, union strategies became geared to the defense of narrow interests in an environment characterized by extensive legal regulation of industrial relations.

The predominant form of dispute resolution is compulsory arbitration by the labor courts, which are empowered to settle both disputes over rights and disputes over the terms and conditions of employment. Excessive emphasis on the law has greatly narrowed the range of issues that remain open to collective bargaining. The CLT requires that all contracts adhere to a set of minimum standards. Individual employment contracts are consequently burdened by regulations, creating rigidities in labor markets. The law also mandates employer payments toward fringe benefits that significantly increase total labor costs (wages plus social benefits).

Hailed as an unprecedented welfare initiative, the social security system was designed to protect workers and their families against destitution as a result of retirement, disability, or the death of the breadwinner. The costs of the benefits were to be covered by a tax on workers' earnings, matched by both their employers and the federal government. Benefits were paid out of a government fund, and the level of pension reflected a worker's past earnings. A compensation system against work-related injuries and occupational diseases was also put into place, again entailing a levy on payrolls. As if to stress the contributory aspect of pensions, eligibility for retirement was made dependent on length of service, not age. In general, men are allowed to retire after thirty-five years on the job and women after twenty-five years.

Corporatism froze old patterns of inequality that stemmed from the concentration of wealth in the cities and the countryside. In a country where workers had been left to fend for themselves, social security and jobs in which workers enjoyed legal protection became a highly valued prize. But entry into the system was restricted to a small fraction of the existing work force—the urban wage earners covered by long-term formal contractual provisions. Until recently, most rural workers were excluded; the burgeoning mass of undifferentiated urban labor still is. Corporatist institutions shaped a strongly segmented labor market at a relatively early stage of industrialization, providing overprotection to core workers in the modern sector at the expense of the underprotection of labor in general.

Governments of all persuasions upheld the commitment, however rhetorical, to extend social protection to the bulk of the population. Meanwhile, the political regulation of market forces continued to produce unequal social and economic outcomes. As unions began to flex their political muscle, legislators eagerly outbid each other to approve new labor rights, such as the payment of an annual bonus (dubbed the thirteenth wage) that accrued mostly to workers in the primary labor market. Unlike unskilled labor, the core work force was able to protect its relative wage position and to win supplemental fringe benefits through arbitration awards or collective bargaining.[4]

The postwar performance of the Brazilian economy made government promises credible. During the heyday of import-substitution-industrialization, from the mid-1940s to the second oil shock of 1979, the rate of growth stayed above 5 percent per year. Led by manufacturing, all sectors of the economy boomed, and a sufficient number of jobs were created. In the 1950s and 1960s, employment grew in tandem with the population; in the 1970s, it surged ahead of population growth. Yet Brazil was never able to create as many "good" jobs—that is, wage employment covered by formal contracts and social protection programs—as were needed, and redundant labor had to be accommodated in the informal sector.

The intensity of industrialization fundamentally transformed Brazil's society and economy. Within a generation, an economy based on agriculture and commerce became an economy focused on the city and industry. The resulting migratory flows transformed what was still a predominantly rural society in 1960 into the predominantly urban society of today. Converging trends in industrialization and urbanization markedly shifted the sectoral distribution of employment, shrinking the share of agriculture. From 1950 to 1990, when the total work force grew from 17 million to 62 million, employment in agriculture grew by only 40 percent, whereas it was multiplied by a factor of 5.8 in manufacturing and construction, 8.5 in commerce, 7.6 in services, and 6.1 in the public sector. Population trends were equally dramatic. From the mid-1940s to the mid-1970s, the Brazilian population tripled. Since the 1980s, fertility rates have decreased by half, with women giving birth to three children on average now. As fertility rates ebbed, however, the number of working women increased sharply. Moreover, children born during the boom years before 1980 are now pouring into the workforce, which is growing by a million each year.

There was a significant downside to this transformation. Jobs for migrants with poor education or little work experience were scarce in big cities, so the number of the poor in urban areas increased. With cities growing at unusual speed, housing became scarce. Educational and health services could not keep up with the demand from this rapidly expanding population.

It took another centralizing regime to adapt the labor and social protection institutions inherited from the 1930s to the reality of an urban mass society. The post-1964 authoritarian regime updated Brazil's corporatist structure, reasserting centralization and pervasive government regulation. Simple demographics, however, made it virtually impossible to sustain the exclusionary features of early corporatism. What emerged over time was a curious mix of drastic action and incremental change that superimposed new social policy strategies on existing structures, producing unintended and often socially undesirable outcomes.

The centralization of policy decisions as well as tax revenues in the hands of the federal government was the key institutional change. The roles of Congress and of state governments in social spending were reversed, reducing intergovernmental relations to a kind of subordinated federalism. To strengthen policy implementation capabilities at the local level while keeping policy decisions tightly under control, the federal government established large revenue-sharing funds (Fundos de Participação de Estados e Municípios), which provided grants according to a formula that gave more money to poorer states and municipalities. New social funds were created to support welfare programs and to provide investment capital for a broad range of federal projects. The FGTS severance pay fund (Fund for the Guarantee of Workers Security), financed by an 8 percent payroll contribution that is returned to the worker as a lump-sum payment upon dismissal, retirement, or disability, became the principal funding source for housing and sanitation development projects. Other funds, such as the PIS/PASEP (Programa de Integração Social/Programa de Apoio à Formação do Patrimônio do Servidor Público) and the Finsocial (Contribuição Social sobre o Lucro Líquido), served similar purposes as revenue-sharing schemes or funding sources for compensatory social programs.

The social security system was thoroughly revamped. The old structure of separate institutes organized along sectoral lines was unified into a vast new National Social Security Institute (INPS), which centralized the provision of retirement pensions, public assistance benefits, and health care nationwide. Centralization was followed by massive entitlement, with social protection veering toward universal coverage. Nearly the entire population was made eligible for government-provided health care, and retirement pensions were extended to the rural workers under the newly created Funrural social security program. To meet rising demand for health care, the federal government resorted to extensive subsidization of private services, creating a system in which government-provided health care and privately purchased medical insurance coexist, and private hospitals and doctors are reimbursed by the government for medical services rendered to the population.

Institutional reform, a successful stabilization program, and an uncommonly favorable international environment paved the way for a period of extraordinarily fast economic growth. From 1967 to 1973, Brazil could boast of an economic miracle in which families and individuals in all income brackets shared. The population below the poverty line dropped from 54 percent in 1970 to 25 percent in 1980.[5] But while poverty declined, the gap between rich and poor widened. The sharp increases in income inequality from 1960 onward resulted to a large extent from changes in human capital that secured large gains for better-educated workers while the incomes of the less educated remained constant.

True to form, spending on education was greatly increased under the banner of universalizing opportunity. An adult literacy program (MOBRAL) was created, and the government announced its intention to provide broader access to schooling. Yet basic education did not become an overriding public policy goal. To meet the rapidly increasing demand for education, public schools were hard pressed to provide the required classroom space and teachers even if it entailed lowering standards and sacrificing the quality of education. A focus on quantitative results and the transfer of control of the education budget from the federal government to state and municipal governments put a premium on student enrollment, school construction, and the adoption of programs to compensate for the effects of impoverished family background, such as a lower ratio of students per teacher and the provision of school lunches. Little or no attention was paid to raising the quality of education through teacher training and increased remuneration, curriculum development, improved school management, or the selection and supply of adequate textbooks. The poor quality of education overall created a vicious circle: public schools have extremely high rates of grade repetition; unable to make progress through the grades, many students stay in school until they are sufficiently discouraged to drop out; unable to enhance student achievement, public schools expend valuable resources on repeaters.[6] Although at present nearly all school-age children begin primary school, less than half finish the eighth-year primary cycle.

The low priority granted to primary schooling contrasted sharply with the high levels of federal spending on public higher education. Although all three tiers of government—local, state, and federal—increased their share of spending for primary and secondary education, nothing quite matched the federal support provided to public universities from 1968 onward. The inequity of public spending on education is nowhere more apparent than at this level, where free tuition and demanding entrance examinations have turned public universities into a haven for middle-class students. A recent study by the World Bank indicated that the poorest 20 percent of the population are allotted 16 percent of total spending on education, whereas the richest 20 percent get a share of 24 percent.[7]

Overall, the expansion of entitlements under authoritarianism left a mixed legacy. Social protections were increased and coverage was greatly extended, but the quality of services declined. Excessive policy centralization and poor oversight created a fertile ground for waste and corruption. Programs were launched not because of their social usefulness but because of opportunities for pork. Competing federal bureaucracies created a large number of compensatory social programs with overlapping jurisdictions and clienteles, while investment in human capital, especially through basic education, lagged. Public assistance programs have often failed to reach the truly needy because they are poorly conceived and implemented. More important, excessive reliance on payroll taxes rather than general taxation made welfare revenues highly vulnerable to the ups and downs of the economic cycle, so that the social security system is careening toward bankruptcy.[8]

CHANGING PATTERNS OF POVERTY AND INEQUALITY

In contrast to the preceding two decades, the 1980s were a period of unprecedented economic adjustment. A deep fiscal and debt-servicing crisis threw the country into alternating short-term cycles of recession and expansion. The growth rate fell sharply from 1981 to 1983, creating the most severe economic crisis since 1929. The recession was followed by a vigorous but short-lived spell of growth that ended with the collapse of the *cruzado* price-wage freeze stabilization plan implemented by the Sarney government in 1986. The trajectory of decline was compounded by the failure to balance the public accounts. Annual inflation rates hovered around 200 percent between 1984 and 1987, jumped to 685 percent in 1988, and spiraled into hyperinflation in 1989. Inflation was halted abruptly by the draconian stabilization measures adopted by the government of Fernando Collor, only to resume shortly thereafter. The cycle of stagflation was not broken until the successful introduction of a new, inflation-free currency, the *real*, in July 1994.

Stagflation broke the paradoxical pattern of rising inequality and decreasing poverty that prevailed between 1960 and 1980. Except at the top, incomes declined in every bracket, especially the lowest (see Table 3.2).

Individuals in the upper echelon of the distribution were able to protect earnings against inflation through daily indexation mechanisms. Highly concentrated industries accommodated union pressures by raising prices, thereby passing hefty wage hikes on to consumers. But rising inflation in a recessive environment had a disastrous impact down the social ladder. Workers in the lower income brackets were hit hard by unemployment, and

Table 3.2   Income Inequality in Brazil, 1960–1990 (percent of economically active population with nonzero incomes)

Deciles	1960	1970	1980	1990[1]
Lowest 20%	3.5	3.2	3.0	2.3
Next 60%	42.1	34.6	30.9	31.6
Upper 20%	54.4	62.2	66.1	66.1
Top 10%	39.7	47.8	51.0	49.7
Top 5%	27.7	34.9	33.8	35.8
Top 1%	12.1	14.6	18.2	14.6
Ratio of +10%/−10%	34	40	47	78

Sources: Compiled from Regis Bonelli and Lauro Ramos, "Income Distribution in Brazil: An Evaluation of Long-Term Trends and Changes in Inequality Since the Mid-1970s," in Rosane Mendonça and André Urani, eds., *Estudos Sociais e do Trabalho,* vol. 1, Rio de Janeiro: Instituto de Pesquisa Econômica Aplicada, 1994, pp. 7–30.
Note: Estimates from IBGE's National Household Surveys (PNADs).

high inflation amplified income inequality by wiping out the savings of middle-income groups and pushing them into poverty.[9]

As their lot worsened, the poor saw their chances for a better life slip through their fingers. In the postwar period, the poor tolerated inequality because of the high rates of social mobility, from one generation to another as well as within the same generation. But intergenerational upward mobility rates dropped from 47 percent in 1973 to 37 percent in 1988. And the probability of moving up the ladder during one's lifetime fell from 54 percent to 27 percent in the same period. Among those trapped in poverty, many sensed that whatever prosperity existed in the country was not for them.[10]

The 1988 constitution aggravated the situation by simultaneously reducing the capacity of government to act and increasing pressures for higher spending. Extensive welfare entitlements, fiscal and regulatory privileges, and labor rights were enshrined within the document. But the urge to devolve power to state and local governments led to a massive transfer of tax revenues from the federal level to states and municipalities without a concomitant transfer of responsibility for the implementation of social policy.

In the early 1990s, the social security system came to the brink of collapse as expenditures outstripped revenues. Persistent fiscal strain led the federal government to adapt to an atmosphere of austerity. Available revenues set an informal limit on all federal spending, regardless of budget appropriations or emerging needs. As the fiscal crisis deepened, retirement pensions were assigned spending priority to the detriment of health care. Federal health care expenditures fell from $12.7 billion in 1989 to 7.4 billion in 1992, wrecking public health care delivery systems. Private insurance became an alternative for those who could afford it. In most public hospitals, however, medical care rationing became the only feasible policy, forcing staff to refuse new admissions and to deny lifesaving treatment to some patients.

The apparent failure of the government's social policy changed public sentiment toward the plight of the poor. In 1993, the Campaign to Feed the Hungry (Campanha Contra a Fome) summoned Brazilians to pitch in to alleviate poverty without the support of government. The call drew an unprecedented response. Out of indignation and compassion, hundreds of thousands of families donated foodstuff and clothes, money, and hours of volunteer work. In a belated attempt to allay negative public opinion, President Itamar Franco set up an emergency program to distribute food baskets to thousands of families in the impoverished northeast, to provide aid to undernourished children and pregnant women, and to decentralize the school lunch program.[11]

Bringing inflation down, however, was the biggest step yet toward reducing poverty. The new stabilization plan cut inflation from an annual rate of about 5,000 percent in early 1994 to 21 percent in 1995. It is mostly the poor who have reaped the benefits of low inflation. It is estimated that from 1994 to 1995 the income share of the poorest half of the population increased 1.2 percent (an upward shift of $7.3 billion), while the share of the top 20 percent fell 2.3 percent (a loss of $12 billion).[12] Economic stabilization has also brought forward new visions for "redeeming the social debt," in which the traditional handout approach to social policy is giving way to suggestions for fundamental change in order to lift people above poverty and to redress inequality.

NEW DIRECTIONS FOR REFORM

"Brazil is no longer an underdeveloped country," said Fernando Henrique Cardoso in his 1994 presidential campaign platform. "It is an unjust country."[13] His efforts to make progress in Brazil are set against a bleak backdrop. Brazil has one of the worst income distributions and least-educated populations among emerging countries of comparable size, and the sheer scale of needed social reform is disheartening. Moreover, the need for constitutional amendments at every step turns change into a cumbersome and enervating process. Yet Cardoso vowed to persevere and to risk losing his popular appeal in pursuit of reform.

In social policy, success depends on the ability to innovate. The core areas of Cardoso's social agenda are employment, education, health, agriculture, sanitation, and housing. His strategy consists of a "creative mix of emergency action programs and structural reforms." He proposes massive investment in human capital aimed at equalizing opportunity and enabling the poor to break out of poverty. At the same time, he considers compensatory policies that provide immediate protection to the poorest and most vulnerable individuals to be an indispensable complement to long-run social investment policies.[14] The Comunidade Solidária is a federal government program that was set up to target pockets of poverty throughout the country. It represents an effort to cut through red tape and bureaucratic inertia in order to expedite the delivery of public assistance and services to the poor. By narrowing its role to the coordination of existing poverty alleviation programs, the Comunidade Solidária has avoided becoming a new appendage to the apparatus of government.

Another key aspect of Cardoso's reform agenda is the recognition that past social programs that were centrally managed by government with almost no outside control were far from successful. Therefore, emphasis is on designing smaller, decentralized programs that are more responsive to market mechanisms and social influence. Moreover, in the past, the government's response to increasing program costs was either to push through new levies or allow the value of the benefits to be eroded by inflation. By focusing on performance, the Cardoso government hopes to make social policy more innovative and cost-effective.

At least as important as the scale of the proposed reforms is the manner in which they are presented. The Cardoso administration's rationale for social reform is to achieve long-term economic efficiency to overcome poverty and promote greater social equality. This will require changes considered by many to be politically unachievable. The rise of deficit reduction to the top of the national agenda means that the country must face a prolonged dose of austerity, living with higher unemployment and leaner social programs while it gets its finances under control. And to open the way for sustained growth, a host of constitutional reforms involving social security, the civil service, labor rights, and the tax system are needed. Predictably, efforts to overhaul the public sector by taking an ax to existing entitlements are likely to harden resistance to change.

Many of Cardoso's coalition partners would rather take an occasional nip out of social spending, hoping to preserve the system essentially intact. They will, however, be put under severe strain as the pace of reform quickens. Therefore, the president will not be able to rely on the size of his popular mandate to achieve his goals but will have to constantly reassess support to engineer a congressional majority.

Education

Hardly anyone disagrees nowadays that basic education is the key to improving the skills and opportunities of the future workforce. It is also agreed that it is the low quality of Brazil's primary and secondary schools, rather than limited access or insufficient funding, that is the main problem. Teacher training and compensation, curriculum development, the selection and distribution of adequate textbooks and school materials, the institution of performance reviews, and an extended school year are seen as effective means to reduce grade repetition and the huge waste of resources this entails. The goal is for upcoming generations to have at least eight years of schooling.

Congress approved in 1996 a constitutional amendment sponsored by the Cardoso administration that will channel most public funds earmarked for education to primary schools. States and municipalities are currently required to spend at least 25 percent of their total revenues on education. The new law provides for only 10 percent of these funds to be spent directly by local governments. The remaining 15 percent would go into a new revenue-sharing fund that would provide grants to municipalities in proportion to the number of students enrolled in primary schools. At least 60 percent of all grant moneys must be spent on improving teachers' salaries.

Reducing federal spending for university education, however, remains a distant goal. Federal universities account for only 22 percent of overall university enrollment but receive 80 percent of all federal spending on education. But Congress has been reluctant to take the ax to such middle-class entitlements as subsidized higher education.

Job Creation and Employment Flexibility

To create the jobs needed to raise average earnings and absorb new entrants into the labor market, Brazil must invest more to develop both physical and human capital. Many contend that the government should do everything in its power to encourage economic growth, regardless of the short-term costs involved. The argument is that getting the economy back on track would do more for the workforce in the long run than any amount of government spending. Opinion surveys conducted in Congress show that job creation through rapid economic growth is viewed by a large majority of legislators (92 percent in 1991 and 82 percent in 1995) as the most effective means for improving social conditions.

It is not the capacity to create jobs but the low quality of the jobs created that is Brazil's main problem. As Cardoso acknowledged, "Cheap labor and abundant natural resources no longer constitute comparative advantages in the new international production model." The key is to improve the skill levels of Brazilian workers through education and training in order to increase productivity and enable them to adapt to rapidly changing technologies and workplace practices. Better educated workers can expect to move up the earnings ladder. However, the premium wages paid to education continue to be a cause for concern. Despite the considerable educational upgrading of the workforce during the 1980s, income inequality continued to rise.[15]

Job creation is also affected by labor market flexibility. The regulatory environment in which firms operate reduces their ability to adapt to economic change and creates an incentive for the expansion of the underground economy. To create more flexible labor-management relations, employees and employers need to adopt collective bargaining to resolve conflicts, rather than depend on government-mandated regulations. Furthermore, two major changes should be made in the current system. First, the legal framework should consist of broad guidelines, not minutely detailed regulations. Second, the labor courts should have jurisdiction over disputes concerning rights, but not disputes over interests.[16] A move toward such arrangements is supported by a clear majority of Congress (82 percent up from 63 percent in 1991). Rigid work regulations contribute to bloated labor costs.

Nonwage costs are, on average, about 102 percent of the basic wage. Too much emphasis on social levies drives many smaller firms out of business or into the informal sector. Nearly 60 percent of legislators agree with a proposal currently before Congress to reduce social levies in order to foster job creation.

In the past decade and a half, there has been an extraordinary increase in the number of employers, which means that small business made a decisive contribution to job creation during the period. But smaller firms face steep barriers to debt and equity financing. The Comunidade Solidária's proposal to provide low-interest loans to cooperatives and small business failed to elicit a positive response from more than 43 percent of legislators. Other flexibility-enhancing proposals for smaller firms are also controversial. Only a third of Congress approves of the removal of restrictive job-protection guarantees for small business (see Table 3.3).[17]

Access to Farmable Land

Land reform has been highly controversial. It is estimated that 58,000 large estates account for about 45 percent of the total farmable land, whereas 2.9 million small and middle-size farms must share a meager 2 percent. There are also millions of acres of idle farmable land. In 1964, the threat of confiscation of private lands along federal highways hastened the overthrow of President João Goulart. The military-sponsored Estatuto da Terra of 1967 sought to modernize agriculture by turning farms into "rural enterprises" and taxing unproductive landed estates out of business. Although the Estatuto altered the context of agricultural policy by encouraging the newly created "rural enterprises" to modernize agricultural practices and to invest to increase production, the progressive taxation of idle land was not put into practice. Sporadic efforts by the federal government to encourage settlement on expropriated farms in areas where an agricultural economy was well established were by and large unsuccessful. The notion that land reform should benefit the largest possible number of people often led to the distribution of plots too small to be economically viable, and the settlement projects failed to expand production, improve living standards, or sustain themselves over the long haul.[18] In the 1970s, the emphasis shifted from the redistribution of privately owned estates to the

Table 3.3   Congressional Views on Inequality and Poverty Reduction
Proposals (percent "very important" or "very effective")

Policy proposals	November 1991	September 1995
Job creation and employment flexibility		
Create jobs through rapid economic growth	92	82
Promote negotiation of labor contracts through collective bargaining	63	82
Reduce social levies	—	58
Provide low-interest loans to cooperatives and small business ("Banco do Povo")	—	43
Exempt small business from compliance with labor law provisions	—	31
Access to farmable land		
Introduce progressive taxation of unproductive lands and support for tenancy and crop-sharing arrangements	83	54
Implement land reform through the redistribution of private landed estates	51	83
Income redistribution		
Establish employee profit-sharing schemes	74	—
Increase minimum wage	49	42
Establish guaranteed minimum income programs for the poor	32	24
Compensatory programs		
Adopt a CIEP-CIAC model of intensive education for poor children	24	—
Target food aid to the poor	40	—
Provide tax exemption for a basic basket of foodstuff products	—	55
Number of respondents:	406	409

Sources: Bolívar Lamounier and Amaury de Souza, *O Congresso Nacional e a Crise Brasileira,* São Paulo: IDESP, November 1991; and *O Congresso Nacional Frente aos Desafios da Reforma do Estado,* São Paulo: IDESP, September 1995.
Note: In 1991, the question was: "To revert the trend toward rising poverty and income concentration should be an important goal for the next years. How important is each of the following policy instruments to improve social conditions in the country in the next four years?" In 1995, it was worded as follows: "Taking into consideration Brazil's social situation in the next three years and the need to keep inflation low, how efficacious is each of the following policy instruments to reduce poverty?"

settlement of public lands on the edge of the Amazon. Some projects, like the "agricultural villages" alongside the Transamazonian Highway, were utter failures. In Rondônia, where the government succeeded in attracting experienced settlers, the results were strikingly positive. But most of the agricultural frontier was settled without public intervention of any kind, and huge estates took hold of the land. Consequently, innumerable bloody conflicts have been waged in the backlands over title to the land or because of the displacement of subsistence farmers by landed estates.

Recent public debate on this issue has been polarized. The left clings tenaciously to an ideology of "agrarian distributivism" that advocates the expropriation and redistribution of private landholdings as the remedy to Brazil's agrarian problems.[19] Those on the other side of the debate believe that land reform is unlikely to increase output or raise rural incomes in what is already a highly productive agricultural economy. Instead of access to farmable land, unproductive land should be heavily taxed and tenancy and crop-sharing arrangements encouraged in order to expand employment and alleviate rural poverty. On such matters, whatever consensus there is appears to be rather thin. Although the majority of legislators tend to align themselves with the progressive taxation policy alternative (54 percent), more than a third (38 percent) lean toward land reform as a means for reducing rural poverty. More important, Congress seems to be less willing to tamper with land tenure patterns than in the past. Between 1991 and 1995, support declined for both the progressive taxation (from 83 percent to 54 percent) and the land reform (from 51 percent to 38 percent) alternatives. Nonetheless, in 1996 Congress approved two bills sponsored by the Cardoso administration to accelerate land expropriation and introduce progressive taxation of unproductive land.

Income Redistribution

Income redistribution schemes generally elicit extreme reactions. While they are viewed by some as a panacea for lifting people out of poverty, others fear that such schemes discourage work and that the attempt to artificially raise the price of labor may ultimately decrease the number of jobs.

One such proposal has been recently voted into law. Drafted by then Senator Cardoso, the employee profit-sharing bill aimed to encourage workplace bargaining over productivity gains. Although it was supported by 74 percent of legislators in 1991, many now believe that the law failed to deliver on its promises. Instead of enhancing performance and a commitment to results, in many places the new regulation fostered rigidity by establishing the payment of an annual bonus regardless of employee contributions to the bottom line, creating a "fourteenth wage."

Proposals to raise the minimum wage have faced mounting resistance in Congress even though it is one of the main redistributive mechanisms envisaged by the 1988 constitution. This is partly due to the fact that pensions are pegged to the minimum wage, hence every hike threatens to unravel the social security system. Moreover, such raises are likely to benefit only a fraction of the work force. Family breadwinners represent a small proportion of minimum wage earners compared to young workers, many of whom are members of middle-income families.[20]

A government subsidy to increase the incomes of the working poor is considered by many to be the best antipoverty program of all. It would provide an income grant to poor working families with children similar to the U.S. Earned Income Tax Credit program. Many legislators are attracted to the idea because it improves the welfare of the poor without enlarging the public bureaucracy. However, opponents contend that such a program would be subject to significant waste and abuse and would inevitably be expanded with little regard for costs.

The realization that a subsidy program might be onerous and difficult to administer did not prevent a number of municipalities from carrying out local experiments. Brasília and Campinas set up programs to help poor families provided they kept their children in school. It is uncertain whether a similar program will be adopted on a national basis. While a guaranteed minimum income bill passed in the Senate in 1994, the Chamber of Deputies has yet to follow suit. The government is reluctant to increase social spending, and congressional support for minimum income programs actually declined from 32 percent in 1991 to 24 percent in 1995.

Compensatory Programs

Existing remedial programs that provide food aid, temporary work, and nutrition and health support for poor children and families have come under sharp criticism in Brazil for failing to have a significant impact on the living standards of the poor. However, the Comunidade Solidária program itself was recently charged with turning compensatory programs into the main focus of public policy in lieu of implementing a broader and more integral strategy for poverty reduction.

Members of Congress tend to be more receptive to public relief or compensatory programs than to efforts to redistribute income or property. One exception to this is the provision of an intensive elementary school experience aimed at improving the skill, health, and nutrition levels of low-income children in order to enhance learning. The CIEP-CIAC model of intensive schooling (Popular Education Integrated Center and Child Assistance Integrated Center), the creation of Rio de Janeiro's former governor Leonel Brizola, appears to have little appeal for Congress. Food aid, especially when viewed as temporary and justified as a social emergency measure, receives support from about 50 percent of legislators. Exempting a basic basket of foodstuffs from taxation has been put forward by the government as an important adjunct to the economic stabilization program.

It is hardly surprising that social policy initiatives to deliver basic services to all or provide relief to the poorest should enjoy broad support across the political spectrum in Congress. Distributive and compensatory programs may increase spending, but they do not threaten vested interests. To redirect social spending, however, the government must tackle existing benefits that go disproportionately to the better-off. Many legislators are likely to balk at reforms seeking to limit or eliminate existing entitlements for fear that they will alienate old allies among opinion makers, organized labor, and the civil service.

Nevertheless, a redesign of the social agenda implies disrupting or greatly restructuring rights and privileges acquired over the course of half a century. Retrenchment is key to reform. The acid test for this government will be how it tries to resolve the fundamental tension between extending social protections to the bulk of the population and scaling back what a narrow sector of society considers to be its acquired rights.

REFORMING SOCIAL SECURITY

Social security represents probably the most troublesome of all public sector reform issues. The system is supposed to provide a social protection net in the form of pensions for retirees, public assistance for the destitute, and health care for virtually the entire population. In a word, it is Brazil's principal income redistribution mechanism.

In practice, the social security system is an overcentralized, poorly managed operation that uses taxes from today's workers to pay the pensions of today's retirees. As it was initially conceived, the system should have been actuarially sound. But it fell short on its promises almost from the beginning. The federal government only occasionally fulfilled the terms of its statutory contribution, raising job-killing payroll taxes to finance growing deficits and relying on inflation to lower the real value of benefits. Widespread entitlement is yet another cause of the ills of the social security system. The 1988 constitution enlarged the population of potential recipients to include nearly 5 million rural workers, regardless of their past contribution to the system.

The current crisis is not solely the result of mismanagement, corruption, or the extension of entitlements without matching contributions. Changing demographics is part of the tale. As the population ages, the ratio of contributors to beneficiaries is bound to undermine the viability of the system. There are now 34 million contributors and 15 million recipients of social security benefits. In 1940, there were thirty active workers for every retiree; today the ratio is 2.3 to one. The value of benefits has been gradually reduced over time as a means of dealing with this problem. However, pension demands will eventually swell beyond the country's capacity to pay for them.

Moreover, the current system tends to perpetuate rather than reduce social inequality.[21] First, informal sector workers receive no pension benefits even though they represent over 50 percent of the workforce. Second, the existence of universal and contributory concepts of entitlement within the same system means that some people are able to claim retirement payments sooner than others. One relic from the past that complicates social security reform is that under the contributory system, men can retire after thirty-five years and women after twenty-five years on the job. This allows beneficiaries to retire, on average, at age fifty-three, whereas under universal social security the individual begins receiving benefits at age sixty-five or later. Last, there is the separate issue of special entitlements, viewed by many as representative of a morally bankrupt system. The fact that civil servants are entitled to retire with full pay creates a wide disparity in the value of benefits paid in the public and private sectors. Public sector pensions average $5,000 monthly in the judiciary branch, $2,700 in the legislative branch, and $1,100 in the executive branch, whereas retirement pensions for private sector workers average only $180.[22]

In 1995, the Cardoso administration unveiled a plan for reforming Brazil's tottering social security system. The proposal, which requires a constitutional amendment, seeks to curb costs, promote equity in entitlements, and increase the efficiency of the social security system as an income transfer mechanism. The government's proposal triggered fiery rhetoric from opponents on both the left and the right. The fact that the social security system is practically bankrupt apparently does not hold sway with many groups that have developed vested interests in the status quo.

Although a draft proposal was defeated in the federal Chamber in early 1996, the government's chances for reforming social security are not negligible. The idea behind the government's reform proposal is to compel Brazilians to work more years or to contribute for a longer period of time to qualify for full pension benefits. In the future, men would be eligible to retire at age sixty-five and women at age sixty. Survey data collected by IDESP in September 1995 show a majority of legislators in favor of combining length of service and age as eligibility criteria for retirement benefits as the country moves toward a new system of entitlements (see Table 3.4). Another goal of the current administration is to bring civil service benefits in line with private sector

---

Table 3.4 **Congressional Views on Social Security Reform (percent in favor)**

Policy proposals	September 1995
Combine length of service and age as eligibility criteria for retirement	69
Set the same eligibility criteria for public and private sector workers	59
Abolish special entitlements (e.g., for schoolteachers, judges, and legislators)	51
Limit the value of retirement pensions paid by the government to a maximum of three times the minimum wage; additional benefits would require contribution to a private pension fund	30

Sources: Bolívar Lamounier and Amaury de Souza, *O Congresso Nacional Frente aos Desafios da Reforma do Estado,* São Paulo: IDESP, September 1995.

workers' benefits as well as to abolish the special entitlements that ensure generous early retirement for a variety of groups. At least half the legislators agree with the government's proposals even though they themselves stand to lose their privileges. Privatizing part of the government's pension program may be a way around the inevitable flattening of retirement pensions caused by rising demand and declining revenues. The government could guarantee the payment of pensions up to the equivalent of three times the minimum wage. Additional benefits would have to be provided through private pension funds. Legislators tend to shy away from supporting such schemes, despite the fact that instituting privately managed individual retirement accounts is bound to boost domestic savings, providing needed investment capital for restoring economic growth.

Even though it is difficult to assess its extent and impact, opposition to planned cuts in pension rights is not to be taken lightly. In a country where a sizable number of individuals benefit from public largesse and where the idea of acquired rights is deeply ingrained, support for structural change is likely to be limited. Many would opt for some tinkering at the edges of the social security system rather than for its overhaul. Breaking the hold of entrenched interests, however, is only part of the reform process. As a new coalition of interests takes root, the social agenda can be focused on the promotion of equal opportunities for all.

SHAPING A NEW SOCIAL AGENDA

Everyone expects stabilization and adjustment policies to affect employment as business structures are rationalized, the size of government is reduced, and the domestic economy becomes more exposed to international competition. Support for such efforts has been granted under the expectation that increasingly competitive market forces will generate jobs and raise wages at a faster rate. The crucial question is whether this will happen fast enough to arrest declining living standards.

Timing is the principal challenge in shaping any new social agenda. The failure to improve employment, earnings, and public services may eventually trigger a backlash against the government's proposed reforms. President Cardoso recently acknowledged as much in denying charges of government inaction on the social policy front: "Society is more and more anxious for results and less and less tolerant as if the social debt could be redeemed in a single year."[23]

The demand for an equitable sharing of the burden of austerity measures has less to do with the suffering of the poor than with the losses in income and living standards suffered by the middle class and formal sector workers. Even though the deficit is trending down, austerity measures are unlikely to be replaced in the near future by measures to boost the economy. This is because in the absence of reform, the government fears that the result might be an ephemeral economic boom followed by an inflationary bust. Therefore, as the impact of austerity measures hits home, support for the Cardoso administration is likely to ebb among the politically influential middle class.

Moreover, the government's claim that low inflation is the most important redistributive mechanism has been oversold. The poor are still poor even if they are no longer relentlessly impoverished by spiraling inflation. Stability also makes meager wages, unstable jobs, poor education and health services, and inadequate housing more visible and less tolerable.

No new social agenda can be implemented in Brazil without revising legal entitlements and imposing new priorities for social spending. Papering over the weaknesses in existing arrangements instead of moving toward fundamental reform only runs the risk of failing to close the gap between the rich and the poor fast enough. President Cardoso appears to be uniquely poised to steer Brazil back onto the road to development and to implement the nation's social agenda. The fact that he has faced unflinchingly the need for direct and more active measures of poverty alleviation through the promotion of social security, education, and land reform bodes well for the future.

NOTES

1. For a detailed description, see Bolívar Lamounier and Amaury de Souza, *O Congresso Nacional e a Crise Brasileira* (São Paulo: IDESP, 1991); *O Congresso Nacional e as Reformas* (São Paulo: IDESP, March 1995); and *O Congresso Nacional Frente aos Desafios da Reforma do Estado* (São Paulo: IDESP-FIESP, September 1995).

2. The debate is reprinted in Amaury de Souza and Bolívar Lamounier, eds., *As Elites Brasileiras e a Modernização do Setor Público: Um Debate* (São Paulo: IDESP, 1992), p. 28.

3. On the 1930 model, see Bolívar Lamounier and Edmar Lisboa

Bacha, "Democracy and Economic Reform in Brazil," in Joan M. Nelson, ed., *A Precarious Balance: Democracy and Economic Reforms in Latin America* vol. 2 (San Francisco: Institute for Contemporary Studies, 1994), pp. 143–185.

4. For a more detailed discussion, see Hélio Zylberstajn and Amaury de Souza, "Structural Adjustment and the Labor Market in Brazil," in Jacques Marcovitch, ed., *Brasil e Índia: Uma Análise Comparativa* (São Paulo: Universidade de São Paulo, Instituto de Estudos Avançados, 1994), pp. 135–152.

5. Individuals are classified as poor if per capita reported family income is equal to or less than one-fourth of the minimum wage adjusted for inflation. The per capita measure removes the effects associated with family size. At present, the poverty line is defined by a monthly income of $28 or less.

6. See Cláudio de Moura Castro, *Educação Brasileira: Consertos e Remendos* (São Paulo: Editora Rocco, 1993); and Alberto de Mello e Souza, "Educational Policies: Efficiency and Equity Issues," *Revista Brasileira de Economia*, vol. 48, no. 4 (October-December 1994): 411–420.

7. See World Bank, *Brazil: A Poverty Assessment* (Washington, D.C.: World Bank, 1995).

8. Payments of rural social security benefits have invariably outstripped contributions by a wide margin. In 1993, the 5.3 million retirement and disability pensions paid to rural workers represented 13 percent of overall social security payments, but rural-based contributions covered only 2.3 percent of the cost.

9. From 1981 to 1991, unemployment and inflation accounted for about one-third of the variation in labor earnings inequality. See Eliana Cardoso, Ricardo Barros, and André Urani, "Inflation and Unemployment as Determinants of Inequality in Brazil: The 1980s," *Texto para Discussão*, no. 298 (Rio de Janeiro: Instituto de Pesquisa Econômica Aplicada, 1993).

10. See José Pastore and Archibald O. Haller, "O Que Está Acontecendo com a Mobilidade Social no Brasil," in João Paulo dos Reis Velloso and Roberto Cavalcanti de Albuquerque, eds., *Pobreza e Mobilidade Social* (São Paulo: Editora Nobel, 1993), pp. 25–49.

11. Targeting the poor was an important policy innovation. To avoid dispersing benefits, the municipalities that should receive the highest priority were selected from previously mapped pockets of poverty. For a detailed description of the *Mapa da Fome*, see Anna Maria T. M. Peliano, "Um Balanço das Ações de Governo no Combate à Fome e à Miséria— 1993," *Documento de Política* (Rio de Janeiro: Instituto de Pesquisa Econômica Aplicada, 1994).

12. Estimates are derived from the 1995 national household survey. See *Carta de Conjuntura* (Rio de Janeiro: Instituto de Pesquisa Econômica Aplicada, March 1996).

13. See *Mãos à Obra Brasil: Programa do Governo Fernando Henrique*, September 30, 1994, p. 3.

14. A provoking discussion of a mix of human capital investment, distributive, and compensatory strategies to tackle the problem of poverty in Brazil is found in Ricardo Paes de Barros, José Márcio Camargo, and

Rosane Mendonça, "Uma Agenda de Combate à Pobreza no Brasil," *Perspectivas da Economia Brasileira 1994*, vol. 1 (Rio de Janeiro: Instituto de Pesquisa Econômica Aplicada, 1994), pp. 117–129.

15. See Regis Bonelli and Lauro Ramos, "Income Distribution in Brazil: An Evaluation of Long-Term Trends and Changes in Inequality Since the Mid-1970s," in Rosane Mendonça and André Urani, eds., *Estudos Sociais e do Trabalho*, vol. 1 (Rio de Janeiro: Instituto de Pesquisa Econômica Aplicada, 1994), pp. 7–30.

16. For a discussion of labor relations reform, see Zylberstajn and Souza.

17. The Cardoso administration recently introduced legislation to allow the widespread use of temporary employment contracts.

18. An excellent overview is found in Yony Sampaio, "A Questão Agrária no Brasil e o Plano de Reforma Agrária do MIRAD," in Antônio Salazar P. Brandão, ed., *Os Principais Problemas da Agricultura Brasileira: Análise e Sugestões* (Rio de Janeiro: Instituto de Pesquisa Econômica Aplicada, 1992), pp. 99–137.

19. For a thoughtful critique of the "agrarian distributivism" argument, see Francisco Graziano Neto, *A Tragédia da Terra: O Fracasso da Reforma Agrária no Brasil* (Araraquara: Universidade Estadual de São Paulo, 1991). It should be emphasized that the 1988 constitution exempted productive landed estates from expropriation for land reform purposes.

20. See Lauro Ramos and José Guilherme A. Reis, "Minimum Wage, Income Distribution, and Poverty in Brazil," *Texto para Discussão*, no. 359 (Rio de Janeiro: Instituto de Pesquisa Econômica Aplicada, 1994).

21. Health care is an important exception. Decentralization and universal coverage became the hallmark of the Unified Health System (SUS) established by the 1988 constitution. The federal government, states, and municipalities are now jointly responsible for the funding and delivery of health care services. Although the state-local sector depends on federal block grants, it is empowered to design its own health care programs.

22. See Hélio Zylberstajn and Maria Helena Zockun, "Os Caminhos da Seguridade Social no Brasil," in Reynaldo Fernandes, ed., *O Trabalho no Brasil no Limiar do Século XXI* (São Paulo: Editora Ltr, 1995), pp. 171–189.

23. *O Estado de São Paulo,* May 6, 1996.

4

The New
U.S.-Brazil Relationship

Susan Kaufman Purcell

Since the inauguration of Fernando Henrique Cardoso as president of Brazil on January 1, 1995, relations between the United States and Brazil have become particularly cooperative and constructive. Although part of the explanation for the improved relationship is a deliberate decision on the part of Presidents Cardoso and Clinton to create a special relationship between Brazil and the United States, the whole explanation is more complex. Even before the election of both presidents, a number of developments, both within Brazil and the United States, as well as in the world at large, had begun to produce greater congruence between the national interests of both countries.

THE END OF THE COLD WAR

The collapse of the Soviet Union and the end of the Cold War are key factors in explaining the general improvement that has occurred in the relations between the United States and Latin America, in general, with the obvious exception of Cuba. During the Cold War, the United States and Latin America often had different priorities. As a superpower engaged in a global struggle against the Soviet Union, the United States viewed developments within Latin America in terms of how they might affect the global balance of power between Washington and Moscow. Latin America, in contrast, wanted to be taken on its own terms. In most cases, it saw itself as peripheral to the Cold War and characterized Marxist movements and revolutionary regimes in the region as primarily home-grown nationalistic phenomena that fed on poverty and inequality. Having had little direct contact with the Soviet Union, Latin America saw U.S. military intervention as the greater threat to its sovereignty. This led even anticommunist governments in the region to call for massive economic rather than military aid programs in order to attack the underlying "causes" of communism in the hemisphere.

These generalizations are less relevant to those countries that were governed by military regimes, particularly in the years immediately following the Cuban revolution. Brazil is included in this category. Fidel Castro's ascent to power and his pursuit of an expansionist revolutionary policy in the hemisphere, aided and abetted by Moscow, initially led to close relations between the United States and the region's anticommunist military governments. During the 1960s, for example, Washington welcomed the Brazilian military coup of 1964 and then provided substantial economic and military aid to the new regime.

With the onset of détente between Washington and Moscow in the 1970s, however, and especially following the election of Jimmy Carter to the U.S. presidency, U.S. relations with Latin America's military governments deteriorated. The main cause was Carter's aggressive human rights policy. Also relevant in the case of Brazil was his interference in the nuclear agreement between Brazil and West Germany.

Events in Grenada, soon followed by the Nicaraguan revolution of 1979—all within the general context of renewed Soviet expansionism—returned Washington to an aggressive anticommunist policy in the hemisphere during the 1980s. In contrast to the early 1960s, this time the threat was perceived as more limited—mainly to Central America and the Caribbean. The onset of the debt crisis in 1982, combined with the beginning of South America's transition to democratic rule, quickly made Washington's renewed preoccupation with security issues in the region even more objectionable than it had been two decades earlier.

The Soviet collapse in 1989 therefore removed a basic cause of friction in U.S.–Latin American relations by allowing Washington to deemphasize security issues and to focus instead on economic ones. At the same time, the end of the communist threat made the granting of massive economic aid to the region a much lower priority in Washington, especially given the large U.S. budget deficit that had developed in the 1980s. Latin America, which had lamented the way in which the Cold War had negatively affected U.S.–Latin American relations, while simultaneously fearing that its end would cause Washington to ignore the region, seemed to have its worst fears confirmed.

THE MOVE TOWARD OPEN ECONOMIES, REGIONAL TRADE BLOCS, AND DEMOCRACY

Fortunately for the future of U.S.–Latin American relations, the end of the Cold War also discredited socialism and gave a big boost to capitalist development strategies, which depended heavily on open economies and free trade. The growing popularity of the computer increased the speed of technological innovation, making foreign investment ever more necessary for developing countries that wanted to develop modern economies. And the scheduled creation of a single European market in 1992 encouraged the United States and Latin America to look toward each other as potential partners in an eventual hemispheric free trade area.

The creation of more open economies throughout Latin America, however, was a necessary, although not a sufficient, stimulus to stronger economic ties between the United States and Latin America. Also important was the redemocratization of the hemisphere. In the absence of a communist threat, Washington would have been considerably less likely to press for free trade agreements with Latin America if the region had continued to be dominated by military governments. As it turned out, both the United States and the newly elected democratic leaders in the hemisphere came to see such agreements as crucial ways of reinforcing democracy and market economies in the region.

Washington initially focused on the rapid implementation of a free trade agreement with Mexico. This reflected not only the shared 2,000-mile border between the two countries but also the desire of the U.S. and Mexican presidents to "lock in" the free market reforms that had been implemented by Mexican president Carlos Salinas de Gortari. Also relevant, however, was the United States' desire to consolidate a North American free trade area as quickly as possible, given the rapid economic integration occurring in Europe, as well as Japan's increasingly close economic ties with Southeast Asia. Next on the U.S. agenda would be Chile, which together with Mexico had achieved the most progress in opening and restructuring its economy.

A free trade agreement with Brazil, in contrast, was not initially a high priority for Washington. Despite the size of its potential market, its strategic location within South America, and its recent transition to democracy, the country lagged considerably behind Mexico and Chile in liberalizing its economy, inflation remained unchecked, and the possible victory of a Marxist labor leader in the 1994 presidential election put Brazil's future economic path in doubt.

The implementation of an economic stabilization program in July 1994, however, which dramatically reduced inflation and helped elect Fernando Henrique Cardoso as president in October 1994 by an impressive margin, strengthened the free trade forces within the government and the country at large. Shortly thereafter, the sudden devaluation of the Mexican *peso* in December 1994 called into question the future of the new development model within Latin America. In that context, the U.S. government began to view Brazil as the new anchor for the reform process in Latin America and, consequently, began to give added emphasis to constructing a cooperative and closer relationship with the Cardoso government.

For its part, the "tequila effect" of the Mexican devaluation had caused foreign investors to withdraw substantial funds from Brazil and other South American countries that seemed to share at least some of the characteristics that were believed to have forced Mexico to devalue its currency. This new situation made a good relationship with the United States more important to Brazil. President Cardoso's April 1995 visit to Washington, and then to New York, where he addressed a luncheon audience of 1,200 business leaders and bankers, was the most visible symbol of Brazil's desire to create a new and better relationship with its northern neighbor.

TENSIONS IN THE
UNITED STATES-BRAZIL RELATIONSHIP

The growing convergence in the interests of the United States and Brazil over the past few years does not imply the absence of important differences between the two governments. In each of the key areas of the bilateral relationship, the interplay of foreign and domestic goals and constraints has produced somewhat different priorities on the part of both Washington and Brasília.

Free trade is a prime example. Both the United States and Brazil are global traders. At the same time, both countries regard Latin America as an important and growing market for their exports. As a result, both governments support free trade agreements within the hemisphere. In early December 1994, for example, the governments of North and South America agreed at the Miami Summit to work for the creation of a Free Trade Area of the Americas (FTAA) by the year 2005.

The building blocks of the FTAA would consist of the existing subregional trade blocs, such as NAFTA, MERCOSUR, the Andean Common Market, Caricom, and the Central American Common Market, as well as other bilateral and trilateral free trade agreements already signed or projected. Each of these agreements, however, had different rules that would have to be reconciled on the road to a hemispheric free trade area. By the time of the Miami Summit, it was already clear that Washington and Brasília had different ideas regarding the integration process.

For the United States, the expansion of NAFTA represented the best way of achieving a Western Hemisphere free trade area. Chile was next in line, but after Chile's incorporation the subsequent steps remained unclear. Although the United States left open the possibility that it would sign free trade agreements with individual Latin American countries, it felt that it would simplify the integration process if groups of Latin American countries first joined together in subregional pacts and then sought entry into NAFTA.

Brazil was unenthusiastic about using NAFTA as the core of a Western Hemisphere free trade area. First, it did not want to encourage a hub-and-spokes integration process, with the United States as the hub and Brazil as merely one of several spokes. Second, Brazil's major non-U.S. trading partners in the hemisphere were not Mexico and Canada but, rather, its MERCOSUR partners, particularly Argentina. Furthermore, Brazil's trade with its MERCOSUR partners was growing faster than its trade with Mexico and Canada. Between 1992 and 1995, for example, Brazil's two-way trade with MERCOSUR expanded about 57 percent. Brazil's two-way trade with NAFTA, while also growing, increased 40 percent during the same period.[1]

As a member of MERCOSUR, Brazil enjoys a competitive

advantage over U.S. exports to the region. This helps explain why Brazilian exports to MERCOSUR increased by an annual average rate of about 40 percent between 1990 and 1994, compared with only a 13 percent increase in the country's exports to the rest of the world over the same period.[2]

Another important explanation for Brazil's desire to consolidate MERCOSUR is the composition of Brazil's exports to the trading bloc. Specifically, South America bought more than 4 percent of Brazil's raw material exports, more than 6 percent of its semi-manufactured exports, "and an astonishing 27.2%" of its manufactured exports—a pattern that is basically reflected by Brazil's exports to MERCOSUR.[3] Stated differently, Brazil's exports to its MERCOSUR neighbors are characterized by "substantial value-added by the Brazilian work force,"[4] in contrast to the predominance of raw materials and agricultural produce that usually predominate in the exports of so-called developing countries.

Brazil would like to maintain its export advantage with MERCOSUR as long as possible, in part to offset the comparative advantage that U.S. exports have over Brazilian ones in the Mexican market. Brazil is also interested in further strengthening MERCOSUR before having it join forces with NAFTA, in order to ensure its survival. Finally, Brazil wants time to consolidate its dominant position within MERCOSUR before having to grant the same advantages to the United States that it now enjoys in its own trade relations with its immediate neighbors in South America.

This partially explains why Brazil originally favored a later deadline for forming a Western Hemisphere free trade area than the 2005 date that was agreed on at the Miami Summit and why Brazilian government officials continue to speak of the 2005 deadline as "tentative."[5] It also accounts for Brazil's decision to work toward the creation of a South American free trade area, with MERCOSUR as its core, as an alternative to merging MERCOSUR with NAFTA. From the Brazilian perspective, it would have a stronger negotiating position vis-à-vis the United States and be treated more as an equal if a Western Hemisphere free trade area were formed by uniting a North American free trade area, dominated by the United States, and a South American free trade area, dominated by Brazil.

The United States has not publicly criticized Brazil's intention of creating a South American free trade area. The Miami Summit declaration left unspecified the process by which a hemispheric free trade area would be formed. This reflects Brazil's influence, since Washington would have preferred a formal acceptance of a process whereby subregional groupings would be incorporated into NAFTA.

It remains to be seen whether the Andean Common Market in particular, which is the other important subregional trade area in South America, will ultimately choose to join NAFTA or to merge first with MERCOSUR. A third possibility, however, is the disintegration of the Andean Common Market. One of its members, Bolivia, already trades more with MERCOSUR than with its Andean partners. In December 1996, it signed a free trade agreement with MERCOSUR that provides for the elimination within ten years of tariffs from nearly all of Bolivia's trade with MERCOSUR. At the same time, Venezuela's trade with northeastern Brazil has been growing rapidly over the past seven years. This has increased both Venezuela's and Brazil's interest in expanding MERCOSUR to include Venezuela, if not as a full member, then as an associate member, modeled after the free trade agreements that Chile and Bolivia have with MERCOSUR.

Interestingly, when Brazil first expressed interest in creating a South American free trade area, there were reasons to doubt whether its goal could be realized anytime soon. Argentina was ambivalent about throwing its lot with MERCOSUR over NAFTA, Chile clearly favored entry into NAFTA over MERCOSUR, and Venezuela was more interested in access to the North American market than the South American market.

The rapid growth of the MERCOSUR market, however, combined with growing signs of opposition within the United States to NAFTA's expansion, at least in the near future, caused Argentina, Chile, and Venezuela to give more importance to their respective ties with Brazil and MERCOSUR.

President Cardoso announced in 1995 that, following the consolidation of a South American free trade area, his next goal would be the negotiation of a free trade agreement with the European Union (EU). In part, he was trying to signal to Europe that the Miami Summit's agreement to establish a Western Hemisphere free trade area by the year 2005 should not be considered a threat to Europe's economic ties to Brazil and MERCOSUR. These ties are important not only to Europe but to Brazil as well. The European Union is Brazil's principal trading partner, absorbing 26 percent of Brazil's exports and accounting for 24 percent of its imports.[6] The president's announcement was also directed at his fellow Brazilians, who want their country to remain a global trader. Finally, the fact that Washington has given higher priority to incorporating Chile over Brazil may have persuaded the Brazilian president to deemphasize the desirability, for now, of a MERCOSUR-NAFTA agreement.

An agreement between the European Union and MERCOSUR was ultimately signed in December 1995, but it was not a full-blown free trade accord. France, Spain, and other European countries that benefit greatly from European Union agricultural subsidies feared that without the subsidies they would not be able to compete with MERCOSUR exports of beef, milk, and wheat.

Washington's position on the EU-MERCOSUR accord, as expressed by former U.S. Secretary of State Warren Christopher, is that it is a positive development "as long as it is a building bloc to free trade." Furthermore, U.S. groups that opposed and continue to oppose NAFTA, such as labor and environmental organizations, are considerably more favorably disposed to a U.S. agreement with the European Union than with MERCOSUR, on the grounds that labor and environmental standards in Western Europe are much higher than in Latin America and therefore do not give European countries an unfair competitive advantage in trade relations with the United States. Others see a North Atlantic free trade agreement as a way of maintaining the traditional U.S. special relationship with Western Europe in the aftermath of the disappearance of the Soviet threat, which, while it existed, helped hold the alliance together.

On the other hand, supporters of a Western Hemisphere free trade area are concerned about the possibility that Brazil's eagerness to enter into a free trade agreement with Europe prior to the consolidation of a hemispheric free trade area might derail the momentum toward hemispheric integration. Even worse, they contemplate the possibility that Brazil might ultimately decide to remain outside a Western Hemisphere free trade area once it succeeded in signing accords with South America and the European Union. This would give Europe a comparative advantage over the United States in South America, a development that would not be welcomed by Washington.

It seems unlikely, however, that Brazil would want this kind of development. Although the European Union is currently Brazil's main trading partner, it will probably not remain in that position for long.[7] This is because Brazil's trade with the United States is not far behind and is growing fast. In 1994, for example, U.S. exports to Brazil grew by 35 percent, reaching $8.1 billion.[8]

They were estimated to reach $9.4 billion by the end of 1995, a 29 percent increase over the preceding year, according to the U.S. Commerce Department.[9] By mid-1996, Brazil's exports to the United States were estimated to have exceeded $10 billion.[10] The United States is Brazil's main supplier, with a market share of 24 percent.[11] Brazil's exports to the United States also increased, but at a somewhat lower rate.[12] Furthermore, 35.4 percent or $34.4 billion of the accumulated foreign investment in Brazil comes from the United States. This is more than triple the total investment from Germany, which is the second-place investor with $10.2 billion.[13] In terms of individual countries, the United States is the largest investor in Brazil, with total foreign direct investment equaling almost $19 billion.[14] Brazil also receives more U.S. investment than any other Latin American country.[15] And U.S. companies still have the largest presence in Brazil. Of the thirty-five largest businesses in Brazil, seven (or 20 percent) are U.S.-owned. No other foreign country owns more than two of the top thirty-five companies.[16]

Finally, a larger share of Brazilian exports to NAFTA countries consists of manufactured and semimanufactured goods than is true of Brazilian exports to the European Union. In 1992, for example, Brazil's exports to Western Europe were basic raw materials. Only 11 percent of NAFTA countries' imports from Brazil, in contrast, were raw materials. At the same time, 21.6 percent of Brazil's exports to Western Europe were fully manufactured goods. The comparable figure for the Brazilian exports to NAFTA countries (mainly the United States) was 30.8 percent.

Stated differently, Brazil's most important exports to Western Europe were "food products, tobacco and beverages, followed by minerals, mostly those used for making steel and aluminum, and basic metals. Most of these items [have an] only relatively modest value-added component from a Brazilian standpoint."[17] The most important Brazilian exports to the North American market, in contrast, were "machinery, food, tobacco, beverages, footwear, followed by minerals, metals and transportation equipment," a list that "is considerably more diversified than the European one and contains items with a much higher value-added component."[18] If the U.S. market is disaggregated from those of Canada and Mexico, the contrast with Brazil's exports to Western Europe is even more striking, since Brazil's main exports to the United States include aircraft, machines, auto parts, transportation equipment, shoes, steel, televisions, and chemicals.[19]

Despite the greater predominance of value-added exports to the North and South American markets, compared with exports to the European Union, there is every reason to conclude that Brazil will want to maintain and improve its trade performance in both Western Europe and the Americas. Since the United States also has no desire to choose between Europe and the Americas, both Washington and Brasília have every reason to avoid zero-sum decisions and, instead, work toward free trade agreements involving Europe and the Americas that are inclusionary as opposed to exclusionary.

Although this would undoubtedly be the most rational course of action for both countries, there is, of course, no guarantee that reason will prevail. The U.S. Congress has so far refused to grant President Clinton fast-track authority, which is needed to advance the cause of free trade in the hemisphere. The Brazilian Congress has not yet posed any serious challenge to President Cardoso's ability to negotiate free trade agreements. On the other hand, the Brazilian Congress has little influence on trade matters. Most of the anti–free trade pressure to date has instead come from São Paulo business groups, from the government bureaucracy, and from some members of Cardoso's cabinet.

Such anti–free trade pressure has been minimal to date. It could increase, however, if the country's economic outlook were to worsen, if unemployment became a major political problem, if high rates of inflation were to return, or if U.S. exports to Brazil continue to increase at a much faster rate than Brazilian exports to the United States. The latter has been the case during the past few years. Between 1990 and 1995, for example, Brazilian exports to the United States grew about 16 percent, while U.S. exports to Brazil grew 67 percent during the same period.[20] As a result, in 1995, Brazil registered a $1.6 billion trade deficit with the United States—following decades of trade surpluses.[21] Therefore, the ability of the United States and Brazil to sustain a cooperative relationship on the issue of free trade is not guaranteed and will depend on whether domestic and international developments create the perception in both countries that the benefits of free trade significantly outweigh the costs.

In addition to the issues surrounding a future hemispheric free trade area, a number of strictly bilateral trade issues remain on the agenda. Brazil has argued that many of its important exports to the United States continue to encounter high tariff or nontariff barriers that keep Brazilian exports to the United States from growing more rapidly. The list includes Brazilian orange juice, tobacco, and gasoline. Much of the earlier friction between the United States and Brazil over trade issues has been eliminated, however, in great part as a result of Brazil's economic opening and restructuring. With the disappearance of import licensing, for example, Brazil was no longer a priority target for trade sanctions under the U.S. trade act of 1974. Conflicts over technology issues have also been reduced with Brazil's opening of its informatics industry and the passage of intellectual property legislation.

Earlier conflict over the transfer of sensitive U.S. technology also has dissipated. Part of the explanation is undoubtedly the end of the Cold War and the increasing consolidation of Brazilian democracy. Also relevant is Brazil's ratification of both an agreement on nuclear safeguards with the International Atomic Energy Agency and the 1967 Tlatelolco Treaty, which bans nuclear weapons in Latin America and the Caribbean. President Cardoso has also said that Brazil may decide to sign the Nuclear Nonproliferation Treaty as well. These decisions were followed by and related to U.S. Secretary of Defense William Perry's visit to Brazil in November 1994, where he called for closer bilateral cooperation between the two countries in the aerospace industry.[22] Secretary of State Warren Christopher's subsequent visit to Brazil in March 1996 resulted in an agreement opening the way for Brazil to buy nuclear technology from U.S. companies.[23]

During Secretary Christopher's visit, the United States and Brazil also signed a new bilateral agreement for cooperation in space that emphasizes the use of technology for research and analysis on the environment.[24] In the past, U.S. efforts to work with Brasília to preserve the Amazon Basin were seen by some groups in Brazil as efforts to infringe on Brazil's national sovereignty. The Cardoso administration, however, has concluded that cooperation with the United States on environmental issues is in the interest of both countries. A reflection of this change in attitude is the agreement between Brazil's Foreign Minister Luiz Felipe Lampreia and Secretary Christopher to cooperate in protecting Brazil's rainforest.

In the area of foreign policy, the issues over which Washington and Brasília disagree are not important enough to threaten the bilateral relationship in any significant way. Within Latin America, Brazil and the United States would both like to see a democratic Cuba, for example. Yet their policies for achieving that goal differ. The United States recently tightened its economic embargo against Cuba, following the shootdown of two private U.S. planes by the Cuban military over international waters. The so-called Helms-Burton law, which penalizes individuals and companies who "traffic" in property that was expropriated from U.S. citizens, has already led to a heightening of tensions between the United States and Brazil. It is likely, however, that Washington and Brasília will "agree to continue to disagree" over Cuba rather than jeopardize their cooperative and mutually beneficial relationship.

Brazil also has lobbied hard for the expansion of the UN Security Council. As one of the largest and most important of the so-called big emerging market countries, Brazil undoubtedly sees itself as a prime candidate for membership in an enlarged Security Council. For its part, the United States has not made its position on the issue clear—specifically whether or not it favors expansion and, if so, whether only by including Japan and Germany or by adding representation from the so-called developing world as well. Where Washington comes out on this issue will undoubtedly have a positive or negative impact on U.S.-Brazil relations.

In general, however, in the aftermath of the Cold War, the prospects are good that the United States and Brazil will be able to cooperate over the main problems facing the hemisphere, such as drugs, the environment, immigration and refugee problems, and border disputes. The recent diplomatic efforts to resolve the long-festering border dispute between Peru and Ecuador is a good example of such cooperation.

CONCLUSION

In conclusion, the future prospects for the further development of the new and much-improved bilateral relationship between the United States and Brazil are good, assuming that there are no radical changes in either country that would call into question the political and economic realities on which the current relationship is based. No matter which party controls the presidency and/or Congress in the foreseeable future, a good relationship with Brazil will remain a high U.S. priority, both for economic and political reasons. In truth, the wide disparities between Republicans and Democrats over U.S. policy during much of the postwar period have mainly disappeared with the end of the Cold War. Furthermore, the absence of a shared border between the United States and Brazil means that their bilateral relationship does not become entangled with domestic political and economic issues and problems as occurs in the U.S.-Mexico relationship.

On the Brazilian side, as long as the country remains democratic and committed to an essentially open economy, conflicts between Brasília and Washington will be manageable. At the same time, however, Brazil's approach to the United States may also become increasingly less coherent.

Until now, foreign policy has been the domain of the Brazilian executive and the foreign ministry. The full press freedom that has characterized Brazil since the end of military rule, combined with the spread of mass communications, will bring about the increasing "democratization" or public participation in the foreign policy making process—much as happened in the United States over the past few decades. Specifically, the role of Congress in the foreign policy making process will increase. As a result, Brazil's foreign policy will come to reflect more the views of its diverse citizens. This means that bilateral relations between the United States and Brazil will increasingly come to resemble the kind of relationship the United States has with other democracies in Europe and Asia. These relations are not without conflict, but those disagreements that do exist do so in the context of a friendly relationship based on shared basic values.

NOTES

I would like to thank Ambassador Celso Amorim, Paulo Henrique Amorim, Sérgio Henrique-Hudson de Abranches, and Albert Fishlow for their helpful comments on earlier drafts of this paper.

1. Gary C. Hufbauer and Barbara Kotschwar, "Going Global," *Hemisfile,* December 1995, p. 7.

2. Ibid.

3. Vera Thorstensen and Ernesto Lozardo, "A Question of Opportunity: Brazil's Strategic Trade Options in a World of Regional Blocs," ISOA Policy Paper no. 1, published by the Institute for the Study of the Americas, William Perry, ed., August 1995, p. 3 (mimeo).

4. Ibid.

5. Speech delivered by His Excellency Pedro Malan, finance minister of Brazil, May 6, 1996, on the occasion of the Twenty-Sixth Washington Conference of the Council of the Americas (mimeo).

6. "Brazil Under Cardoso: Returning to the World Stage?" in *Instituto de Relaciones Europeo-Latinoamericanas* (IRELA), Dossier 52, Madrid, January 1995, p. 10.

7. Thorstensen and Lozardo, pp. 3, 21.

8. Thorstensen and Lozardo, p. 13, and Hufbauer and Kotschwar, p. 7.

9. Ian Katz and Joachim Bamrud, *U.S. Latin Trade,* January 1996, pp. 12–13.

10. "Trade by Area," *Boletim do Banco Central do Brasil,* October 1996.

11. "Big Emerging Markets in Latin America," *Business Latin America,* August 1995, p. 12.

12. Speech given by His Excellency Ambassador Luiz Felipe Palmeira Lampreia, minister of external relations of Brazil, at the Council on Foreign Relations, April 19, 1995.

13. Katz and Bamrud, pp. 12–13.

14. "Big Emerging Markets in Latin America," p. 12.

15. Address by His Excellency Fernando Henrique Cardoso, president, Federative Republic of Brazil, at the Sheraton New York, August 19, 1995.

16. Katz and Bamrud.

17. Thorstensen and Lozardo, p. 12.

18. Ibid; and "Brazil: Trade Balance," *Oxford Analytica Daily Brief,* April 4, 1996.

19. Luiz Carlos Bresser Pereira and Vera Thorstensen, "From MERCOSUR to American Integration," in *Trade Liberalization in the Western Hemisphere,* IDB/ECLAC, Washington, D.C., 1995, pp. 413-435.

20. "Brazil: Trade Balance."

21. José Augusto Guilhon Albuquerque, "Relações Brasil-Estados Unidos e a Integração Continental," *Política Externa,* vol. 5, no. 1 (June 1996): 1–19.

22. IRELA, p. 33.

23. *New York Times,* March 3, 1996, p. 11.

24. Paulo Tarso Flecha de Lima, "Christopher Returns to Brazil," *Brazil File,* vol. 5, no. 3 (April 1, 1996): 7.

Appendix A:
Chronology of Brazilian History

1500   Pedro Alvares Cabral, Portuguese navigator, claims Brazil for Portugal.

1531   Permanent colonization begins.

1580–1640   Spain governs Portugal and its colonies.

1646   Brazil is declared a principality by the Portuguese throne.

1695   Gold is discovered in Minas Gerais.

1750–1777   Marquis de Pombal, prime minister of Portugal, introduces economic reforms.

1763   Rio de Janeiro becomes the capital of Brazil.

1808   Under British protection, the Portuguese royal family moves to Brazil following Napoleon's invasion of the Iberian peninsula.

1822   Brazil declares its independence from Portugal.

1831   Peter I, first emperor of Brazil, abdicates and returns to Portugal.

1840   Peter II is declared emperor of Brazil.

1865   The Triple Alliance of Brazil, Argentina, and Uruguay declares war on Paraguay, which lasts until 1870.

1888   Slavery is abolished in Brazil.

1889   The empire is overthrown in a military coup d'état.

1889–1930   Brazil is governed by state oligarchies, with São Paulo and Minas Gerais as the most powerful actors.

1930   Getúlio Vargas leads a bloodless movement to end the Republic.

1930–1937   Vargas governs Brazil, first as provisional and then constitutional president.

1937–1945   Vargas rules as dictator.

1946   A new constitution restores democracy.

1960   Brasília is inaugurated as the new capital city.

1964   Military overthrows President João "Jango" Goulart.

1964–1985   Military governments rule Brazil.

1985   Constitutional democracy is restored with the selection of Tancredo Neves as president; Neves dies soon after and is succeeded by his vice president, José Sarney.

1986   The *Cruzado* Plan, a heterodox economic shock program, is attempted and fails.

1987   Brazil declares a unilateral moratorium on its foreign debt.

1988   A new constitution is promulgated.

1990   Fernando Collor de Mello is elected Brazilian president.

1992   Faced with impeachment on charges of corruption, Collor de Mello resigns and is succeeded by his vice president, Itamar Franco.

1993   Finance Minister Fernando Henrique Cardoso announces his government's new economic program.

1994   The *Real* Plan is implemented and inflation drops sharply; as a result of the success of the *Real* Plan, Cardoso is elected president in late 1994.

1995   Fernando Henrique Cardoso is inaugurated as constitutional president of Brazil for a four-year term.

Appendix B: Study Group Sessions and Participants

Susan Kaufman Purcell and Riordan Roett, group codirectors
Stephanie Crane, rapporteur

First Meeting - June 14, 1995: "Brazilian Politics at Century's End"
Commentator:
> Riordan Roett, director, Latin American Studies Program, Paul Nitze School of Advanced International Studies (SAIS), Johns Hopkins University

Discussants:
> Sérgio Henrique-Hudson de Abranches, executive director, Sócio Dinâmica Aplicada (SDA), Rio de Janeiro
> Kenneth Maxwell, senior fellow, Latin American Studies Program, Council on Foreign Relations

Second Meeting - October 5, 1995: "Is the *Real* Plan for Real?"
Commentator:
> Carlos Langoni, president, Projecta Consultoria Financeira S/C Ltda., Rio de Janeiro

Discussants:
> Albert Fishlow, senior fellow for economics, Council on Foreign Relations
> Celso Martone, partner, Macro Consultoria Econômica S/C Ltda., São Paulo

Third Meeting - November 29, 1995: "Redressing Inequalities: Brazil's Social Agenda at the Turn of the Century"
  Commentator:
      Amaury de Souza, senior research fellow, Institute of Social, Economic, and Political Research, São Paulo

  Discussants:
      Claudio de Mora Castro, chief of Social Programs Division, Inter-American Development Bank

Fourth Meeting - March 7, 1996: "The New U.S.-Brazil Relationship"
  Commentator:
      Susan Kaufman Purcell, vice president, Americas Society

  Discussants:
      William Rogers, Arnold & Porter
      Celso Amorim, permanent representative of Brazil to the United Nations
      Diego Ascencio, Ascencio & Associates

Study Group Participants
      John M. Abbott, International Monetary Fund
      Ana Maria Amorim, Permanent Mission of Brazil to the United Nations
      David Asman, *Wall Street Journal*
      John Avery, Americas Society
      Stephanie Bell-Rose, Andrew W. Mellon Foundation
      Everett Ellis Briggs, Americas Society
      Eduardo Cabrera, Merrill Lynch & Co., Inc.
      Peter V. Darrow, Mayer, Brown & Platt
      Arminio Fraga, Soros Fund Management
      Francisco Gros, Morgan Stanley & Co.
      Marc Levinson, *Newsweek*
      Luis R. Luis, Scudder, Stevens & Clark
      Bruce Macphail, Wyeth-Ayerst International, Inc.
      David Malpass, Bear Stearns & Co.
      Walter Molano, Credit Suisse First Boston Corp.
      Martha Muse, Tinker Foundation, Inc.
      Mary Anastasia O'Grady, *Wall Street Journal*

Brian D. O'Neill, Chase Manhattan Bank
Alexandre Parola, Embassy of Brazil
John E. Pearson, *Business Week*
Maxwell Pereira, Banco Economico
Arturo Porzecanski, ING Capital Holdings
John Purcell, Salomon Brothers, Inc.
Luis Rubio, Centro de Investigación para el Desarrollo, A.C. (CIDAC)
Nicole C. Sierra, Merrill Lynch & Co., Inc.
Ricardo Silvagni, Price Waterhouse
Dorothy Meadow Sobol, Federal Reserve Bank of New York
Paulo Sotero, *O Estado de São Paulo*
Alan Stoga, Zemi Investments, L.P.
Carmen Suro-Bredie, U.S. Department of State
Stephen Thompson, U.S. Department of State
Thomas J. Trebat, Citibank
Scott Wallinger, Westvaco Corporation
Richard Weinert, Leslie, Weinert & Co., Inc.
Rosemary Werrett, Latin American Information Services

Selected Bibliography

Bacha, Edmar L., and Herbert S. Klein, eds. *Social Change in Brazil, 1934–1985: The Incomplete Transition.* Albuquerque: University of New Mexico Press, 1989.

Baer, Werner. *The Brazilian Economy: Growth and Development,* 4th ed. Westport: Praeger, 1995.

Cardoso, Eliana, and Albert Fishlow. *Macroeconomia da Divida Externa.* Rio de Janiero: Editora Brasiliense, 1988.

Fauriol, Georges, and Sidney Weintraub. "U.S. Policy, Brazil, and the Southern Cone." *Washington Quarterly* 18, no. 3 (summer 1995): 123–131.

Fontaine, Pierre-Michel. *Race, Class, and Power in Brazil.* Los Angeles: University of California Press, 1985.

Franco, Gustavo. *O Plano Real e Outros Ensaios.* Rio de Janiero: Francisco Alves, 1995.

Goodman, David, and M. R. Radclift. *From Peasant to Proletarian.* Oxford: Basil Blackwell, 1981.

Harbison, Ralph W., and Eric A. Hanushek. *Educational Performance of the Poor: Lessons from Rural Northeast Brazil.* New York: Oxford University Press, 1992.

Lamounier, Bolívar. "Brazil: Inequality Against Democracy." In Larry Diamond, Juan J. Linz, and Seymour Martin Lipset, eds. *Democracy in Developing Countries: Latin America,* vol. 4. Boulder: Lynne Rienner, 1989, pp. 119–169.

Lamounier, Bolívar, and Edmar Bacha. "Democracy and Economic Reforms in Brazil." In Joan M. Nelson, ed., *A Precarious Balance: Democracy and Economic Reforms in Latin America and Eastern Europe,* vol. 2. San Francisco: Institute for Contemporary Studies, 1994.

Malloy, James L. *The Politics of Social Security in Brazil.* Pittsburgh: University of Pittsburgh Press, 1979.

Maybury-Lewis, Biorn. *The Politics of the Possible: The Brazilian Rural Workers' Trade Union Movement, 1964–1985.* Philadelphia: Temple University Press, 1994.

Morley, Samuel A. *Labor Markets and Inequitable Growth: The Case of Authoritarian Capitalism in Brazil.* Cambridge: Cambridge University Press, 1982.

Ozorio de Almeida, Anna Luiza, and João S. Campari. *Sustainable*

Settlement in the Brazilian Amazon. New York: Oxford University Press, 1995.

Page, Joseph A. *The Brazilians.* Reading, Mass.: Addison-Wesley, 1995.

Pastore, José. *Inequality and Social Mobility in Brazil.* Madison: University of Wisconsin Press, 1982.

Roett, Riordan. *Brazil: Politics in a Patrimonial Society,* 4th ed. Westport: Praeger, 1992.

Schneider, Ronald M. *Brazil: Culture and Politics in a New Industrial Powerhouse.* Boulder: Westview Press, 1996.

Stepan, Alfred, ed. *Democratizing Brazil: Problems of Transition and Consolidation.* New York: Oxford University Press, 1989.

Werneck, Rogerio. "The Changing Role of the State in Brazil." Texto para Discussão PUC-RJ no. 337, July 1995.

Wood, Charles H., and José Alberto Magno de Carvalho. *The Demography of Inequality in Brazil.* Cambridge: Cambridge University Press, 1988.

World Bank. *Brazil: A Poverty Assessment.* Washington, D.C.: World Bank, 1995.

The Contributors

Amaury de Souza is a senior research associate at the Instituto de Estudos Econômicos, Sociais e Políticos de São Paulo (IDESP), an independent political and economic policy research center. He is also senior partner of Techne, a consulting firm in Rio de Janeiro. He graduated in sociology and administration and holds a Ph.D. in political science from the Massachusetts Institute of Technology. His book *The Politics of Population in Brazil,* coauthored with Peter McDonough, was published in 1981. Recently published papers include "Dilemmas of Industrial Relations Reform: Learning from Brazil's Interest Representation Experience," in Stephen Friedman and Rene de Villiers, eds., *Brazil and South Africa: Comparative Perspectives,* 1996.

Albert Fishlow is a senior fellow for economics, Council on Foreign Relations. He was professor of economics at the University of California at Berkeley until 1994, and the first dean of International and Area Studies from 1990 to 1993. Fishlow served as deputy assistant secretary of state for inter-American affairs in 1975–1976 and has been a member of many public task forces related to Latin American affairs. He is on the board of the Social Science Research Council and serves as chair of its executive committee. His research has addressed issues in economic history, Brazilian and Latin American development strategy, economic relations between industrialized and developing countries, and the problem of foreign debt. Among his recent publications is "NAFTA: What Kind of Future?" in Gerry Helleiner, et al., *Poverty, Prosperity and the World Economy,* 1995.

Susan Kaufman Purcell is vice president of the Americas Society in New York City. Between 1981 and 1988, she was a senior fellow and director of the Latin American Project at the Council on

Foreign Relations. Between 1980 and 1981, she was a member of the U.S. State Department's Policy Planning Staff, with responsibility for Latin America and the Caribbean. A former professor of political science at the University of California, Los Angeles, Purcell holds a Ph.D. from Columbia University. She is a director of Valero Energy Corporation, the Latin American Dollar Income Fund, the Scudder World Income Opportunity Fund, and the Argentina Fund and a board member of the National Endowment for Democracy and of Freedom House. She also serves on the editorial boards of *Journal of Democracy, Journal of Inter-American Studies and World Affairs,* and *Hemisfile.* Her publications include *Europe and Latin America in the World Economy* (editor and coauthor) and *Japan and Latin America in the New Global Order* (editor and coauthor).

Riordan Roett is the Sarita and Don Johnston Professor of Political Science and director of the Latin American Studies Program at the Johns Hopkins Paul H. Nitze School of Advanced International Studies in Washington, D.C. From 1983 to 1985, Roett served as a consultant to the Chase Manhattan Bank in various capacities; from 1993 to 1995 he was the senior political analyst in the Emerging Markets division of the International Capital Markets group. He currently serves as a senior adviser to the World Economic Forum in Geneva and is involved in the planning of the annual meeting in Davos. Roett is a member of the board of directors of seven closed-end funds in New York, including Salomon Brothers Global Partners Income Fund, Worldwide Income Fund, 2008 Worldwide Dollar Government Term Trust, and Emerging Markets Floating Rate Fund. He is a member of the Council on Foreign Relations in New York and is a former national president of the Latin American Studies Association (LASA). Among his publications are *Brazil: Politics in a Patrimonial Society,* 4th ed.; *Paraguay: The Personalist Legacy* (coauthor); and *The Mexican Peso Crisis: International Perspectives* (editor and coauthor).

Index

113

About the Book

Since the inauguration of Fernando Henrique Cardoso as Brazil's president in January 1995, the country has progressed steadily toward creating a more open economy and a more institutionalized democracy, although much still remains to be done. *Brazil Under Cardoso* examines efforts to make Brazil's economy more competitive, its politics more democratic, and its social structure more equitable. The authors also consider the implications of Brazil's reform process for the future of bilateral relations between Brazil and the United States.